GHT BRIEFING FOR PILOTS

VOLUME IV

ASSOCIATED GROUND SUBJECTS

By the same Authors

FLIGHT BRIEFING FOR PILOTS, VOLUME I
An Introductory Manual of Flying Training
Complete with Air Instruction

FLIGHT BRIEFING FOR PILOTS, VOLUME II
An Advanced Manual of Flying Training
Complete with Air Instruction

FLIGHT BRIEFING FOR PILOTS, VOLUME III
Radio Aids to Air Navigation

A GUIDE TO AIRCRAFT OWNERSHIP

THE TIGER MOTH STORY

Direction of take-off and landing may differ. A black ball will be suspended from the signal mast when landing and take-off directions may differ.

The special rules for air traffic in vicinity of aerodromes open to public use not in force. Permanently displayed at all R.A.F. aerodromes.

Special care necessary in landing owing to temporary obstruction or for other reason.

Landing prohibited.

This signal confined to R.A.F., R.N. and M.O.S. aerodromes. Emergency landings only. Normal facilities not available.

Circuits or partial circuits must be right-handed. Keep movement area on the right. A green flag is flown on the signals mast showing pilots on the ground that a right-hand circuit is in operation.

FLIGHT BRIEFING
FOR PILOTS

VOLUME IV

ASSOCIATED GROUND SUBJECTS

BY

N. H. BIRCH

F.R.MET.S.
Director Hamilton Birch Aviation Ltd
Liveryman of the Guild of Air Pilots and Air Navigators

AND

A. E. BRAMSON

Member of the Panel of Examiners
Liveryman of the Guild of Air Pilots and Air Navigators

ILLUSTRATED BY A. E. BRAMSON

Pitman Publishing

First published 1968
Reprinted 1969
Reprinted (*with amendments*) 1970
Reprinted 1972

SIR ISAAC PITMAN AND SONS LTD.
Pitman House, Parker Street, Kingsway, London, WC2B 5PB
P.O. Box 46038, Portal Street, Nairobi, Kenya

SIR ISAAC PITMAN (AUST.) PTY. LTD.
Pitman House, Bouverie Street, Carlton, Victoria 3053, Australia

PITMAN PUBLISHING CORPORATION (S.A.) PTY. LTD.
P.O. Box 11231, Johannesburg, Transvaal, S. Africa

PITMAN PUBLISHING CORPORATION
6 East 43rd Street, New York, N.Y. 10017, U.S.A.

SIR ISAAC PITMAN (CANADA) LTD.
495 Wellington Street West, Toronto 135, Canada

THE COPP CLARK PUBLISHING COMPANY
517 Wellington Street West, Toronto 135, Canada

©

N. H. Birch and A. E. Bramson

1968

ISBN: 0 273 41177 2

MADE IN GREAT BRITAIN AT THE PITMAN PRESS, BATH
G2—(A.204:71)

Contents

Plates 1–8 (Clouds) are positioned between pp. 36 and 37.
Folded inset (Maps 1 and 2) is positioned between pp. 114 and 115.
Front and back endpapers contain ground signals and navigation lights.

Preface

The basis of successful flying instruction is vested in a thorough knowledge of all the related ground subjects. This fourth volume in the *Flight Briefing for Pilots* series should therefore be studied during the early stages of the flying programme or preferably before the flying exercises have begun.

In effect this book is a companion to *Flight Briefing for Pilots*, Volume I, the Introductory Manual of Flying Training and, whenever possible, subjects relating to another chapter or volume are cross-referenced.

Volume IV is intended to provide the student with a basic knowledge of ground subjects which will enable him to pass the Department of Civil Aviation examination for the Private Pilot's Licence while at the same time acting as a first step towards the Commercial Pilot's Licence and/or Flying Instructor's Rating.

N.H.B.
A.E.B.

ACKNOWLEDGEMENT

In writing this book as a successor to *Student and Private Pilot's Handbook* we should like to pay tribute to its author, Mr. H. H. Edwards, for his valuable contribution to civil flying training. In particular, we would acknowledge that some parts of his treatment of Navigation have been included, in modified form, in our interpretation of this Chapter.

NOTE TO 1970 REPRINT

Added to this reprint is a section on the IMC Rating, beginning on page 127.

List of Abbreviations

Ac	. .	altocumulus
A/H	. .	alter heading
a.m.s.l.	.	above mean sea level
As	. .	altostratus
A.T.A.	.	actual time of arrival
A.T.C.C.	.	Air Traffic Control Centres
C	. .	centigrade
C. of A.	.	Certificate of Airworthiness
Cb	. .	cumulonimbus
Cc	. .	cirrocumulus
Ci	. .	cirrus
Cs	. .	cirrostratus
Cu	. .	cumulus
Dev.	. .	deviation
D.R.	. .	dead reckoning
E.T.A. .	.	estimated time of arrival
E.T.D.	.	estimated time of departure
F.I.R. .	.	flight information regions
g.p.h. .	.	gallons per hour
G/S	.	ground speed
Hdg	.	heading
Hdg.(C)	.	heading compass
Hdg.(M)	.	heading magnetic
Hdg.(T)	.	heading true
h.p.	. .	horse-power
ht	. .	height
I.A.S. .	.	indicated air-speed

I.C.A.O.	.	International Civil Aviation Organization
I.F.R.	.	instrument flight rules
I.M.C.	.	instrument meteorological conditions
km	.	kilometre
kt	.	knot
lb	.	pound
M	.	magnetic
m	.	mile
mb	.	millibar
m.p.h.	.	miles per hour
m.s.l.	.	mean sea level
n.m.	.	nautical mile
"Notams"	.	Notices to airmen
Ns	.	nimbostratus
P	.	port
p.p.	.	pin-point
posn.	.	position
R.A.S.	.	rectified air-speed
Reqd. Tr.	.	required track
R/T	.	radiotelephony
S., stb.	.	starboard
Sc	.	stratocumulus
s/h	.	set heading
St	.	stratus
st. m.	.	statute mile
T	.	true (direction, speed)
T.A.S.	.	true air-speed
Tr.	.	track
T.M.G.	.	track made good

var.	.	variation
V.F.R.	.	visual flight rules
V.M.C.	.	visual meteorological conditions
W/V	.	wind velocity

CHAPTER 1

Piston Engines

THE structural and aerodynamic problems associated with heavier-than-air flight have been known to man for centuries and as long ago as 1790 Sir George Caley was able to formulate many of the principles of flight with such accuracy that the results of his experiments bear modern examination.

Although many of the early aeronautical thinkers envisaged man-powered flight (or even bird-powered flight), from the beginning of his long period of research Sir George Caley recognized that the key to success lay in the discovery of a suitable engine. At the time steam was both low powered and cumbersome and the gunpowder engine proved a blind alley. During the eighteenth century engineering techniques were limited so that experiments with hot-air engines proved unsuccessful although in many ways this type of prime mover may be regarded as the link between steam and the modern internal combustion engine which more or less overnight made petrol, hitherto regarded as of little value, into the life's blood of industrial nations.

While it is not necessary for the pilot to have a deep technical knowledge of the theory and design of the petrol engine it is nevertheless important that he should understand the basic principles of the power plant in his aircraft.

Principle

The piston engine produces power by converting fuel (petrol or diesel oil) into heat and heat into energy. The energy is collected by mechanical means and the resultant power transmitted by a rotating shaft which is linked to the driving wheels of a car or made to rotate a propeller in a boat or aeroplane.

It is self-evident that when ignited a liquid fuel will burn and produce heat but how the heat is able to provide mechanical energy will be less obvious until it is realized that heat can be applied to air. When heated, air will expand very considerably exerting great pressures if contained in any way.

Method
To provide perfect combustion in the engine petrol and air must be mixed to a ratio of approximately fifteen parts of air

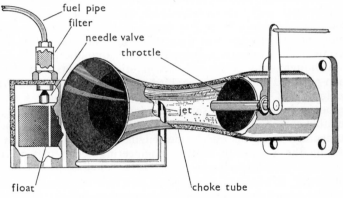

Fig. 1. SIMPLE CARBURETTOR

to one part of petrol by weight. Too much petrol causes a **rich** mixture (which may be recognized by black exhaust smoke). This is both wasteful of fuel and damaging to the engine because heavy carbon deposits build up in the combustion areas. Conversely too little petrol in relation to air causes a **weak** mixture. This, too, is damaging to the engine for instead of the mixture burning at an even rate on ignition an explosion occurs causing severe strain on the engine accompanied by overheating and loss of power. In most piston engines fuel is mixed with air in the **Carburettor**, a simple example being illustrated in *Fig.* 1.

Fuel from the aircraft tanks is pumped to the carburettor

and enters a device similar in design to a domestic w.c. cistern called a **Float Chamber**, the function of which is to maintain the fuel at the correct level in the **Jets**. These jets create an atomizing action rather similar to that of the nozzle of a scent spray. It is usual to provide a **Slow Running Jet** for the purpose of engine idling and a **Main Jet** for normal operation. On some carburettors when the throttle is opened for maximum power an additional **Power Jet** is brought into operation. A reduction in air density will occur as the aircraft gains altitude and since this would result in an over rich fuel/air mixture the carburettor is provided with a **Mixture Control**. An adjustable valve or **Throttle Butterfly** is positioned between the jets and the engine and linked to the pilot's throttle control so that the amount of mixture entering the engine may be regulated, this in turn determining the power output to the propeller.

Feeding the Mixture to the Engine
When the correct mixture for various conditions of height and power setting has been produced it must be transferred to the engine for combustion. As the term implies internal combustion means that the mixture is burned within the engine proper as opposed to steam engines where fuel is consumed under a boiler and the resultant steam transferred to the engine.

In most car and light aircraft engines the petrol/air mixture is inhaled by the engine which in many respects is similar in layout to a bicycle pump. Put into simple terms a **Piston** is arranged to slide up and down within a **Cylinder** which is closed at one end. There must be sufficient clearance between the walls of the cylinder and the sides or **Skirt** of the piston to allow for metal expansion as the engine reaches its working temperature. At the same time a gas-tight fit must be maintained and the piston is therefore provided with a number of **Piston Rings** for the purpose. The rings are made of a high quality springy cast iron so that they press lightly against the cylinder walls. They are split to allow for expansion.

During starting the piston is drawn down the cylinder when the resultant decrease in pressure causes the engine to suck in mixture from the carburettor through an **Inlet Valve** provided for the purpose in the **Cylinder Head**. This phase of the operating cycle is known as the **Induction Stroke**.

Early in the development of the petrol engine it was found that power could be greatly increased if the mixture charge was compressed in the cylinder prior to combustion and the next phase is called the **Compression Stroke**. The inlet valve remains closed during this stroke and the piston moves to its uppermost position compressing the mixture into a small area of the cylinder head called the **Combustion Chamber**. The degree of compression is referred to as the **Compression Ratio,** this being the ratio between the compressed volume (referred to as 1) and the volume of mixture before compression. Thus a compression ratio of 6:1 means that six volumes of mixture are compressed into one volume.

While high compression ratios yield extra power, special fuels are needed to prevent **Detonation**, i.e. explosion after the engine ignites the mixture. Detonation may be recognized as the familiar "pinking" experienced when a car is made to pull hard in top gear while operating on low grade fuel. There is a tendency in design towards higher compression ratios both in car and aeroplane engines and while 6:1 was once considered average 8:1 or even 10:1 is now not uncommon. As a guiding principle the higher the compression ratio the higher must be the lead content of the fuel. This is expressed as an **Octane Number** and the pilot must ensure that the correct grade of fuel is put into the tanks of his aircraft since too low an octane rating will produce detonation while too high a rating may damage the cylinders and exhaust valves.

Having inhaled a charge of mixture (stroke 1) and then compressed it (stroke 2) the engine is now ready to produce power by burning the mixture, the resultant heat expanding the already compressed air.

The mixture is ignited by a **Sparking Plug** which is situated in the cylinder head. At the appropriate time a high tension current generated by the **Magneto** (or ignition coil in a car) is led to the plug causing a spark to jump across its electrodes and ignite the fuel/air mixture. The combustion that follows is not to be confused with an explosion (a sudden release of energy) but it should be imagined as a progressive burning of the fuel, spreading within the combustion chamber like the water ripple which results when a stone is dropped into a pond. The spreading flame heats the air, creating very high pressures within the confines of the cylinder head, and the expanding gas forces the piston down the cylinder with a great deal of energy. This third phase is known as the **Power** or **Ignition Stroke**.

The cylinder is now full of burned mixture (carbon monoxide gas) which has to be removed before a fresh charge can be sucked in for another power stroke and the piston must again travel up the cylinder forcing out the hot gases through the **Exhaust Valve** which is situated in the cylinder head adjacent to the inlet valve. On completion of the fourth stroke the engine is ready to begin the cycle again. From the foregoing it will be seen that in the **Four-stroke** engine described four strokes occur in a complete cycle and although **Two-stroke** engines (which dispense with the use of mechanically operated inlet and exhaust valves) are in everyday use the principle is confined to engines of smaller capacity than those found in most aircraft.

It is of course necessary to convert the up-and-down or **reciprocating** motion of the piston to a rotary movement of the propeller shaft. Additionally a mechanism must be provided to open and close the inlet and exhaust valves at the correct time and a high tension current has to be switched to the sparking plug when the compressed mixture is ready for ignition so it is now appropriate to consider this simple engine in greater detail. The student will by now have noticed that most terms relating to engines are both descriptive and self-explanatory.

Provision of Rotary Motion

In a bicycle the reciprocating motion of the rider's legs is transmitted to the crank via a pair of pedals so converting an up-and-down motion into a rotation which is transmitted by a chain to the rear wheel. In a piston engine (petrol, diesel or steam) the crank and pedals are replaced by a **Crankshaft** and the "legs" of the engine are provided by a **Connecting**

Rod which links the crankshaft to the piston (the muscles of the leg). To allow for the sweeping motion of the crankshaft as it rotates within its **Crankcase** provision is made for the connecting rod to pivot on a **Gudgeon Pin** inserted across the

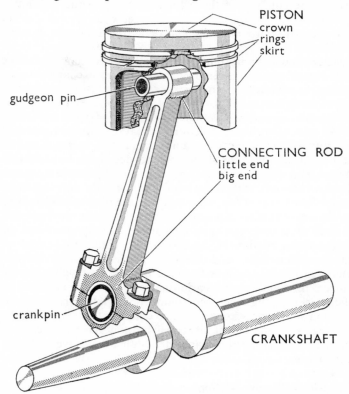

Fig. 2. PISTON, CONNECTING ROD AND CRANKSHAFT
ASSEMBLY

axis of the piston. The pin passes through the **Small End** of the connecting rod and the **Crank Pin** (equivalent to the pedals on a bicycle) is free to rotate in the connecting rod **Big End** bearing (*Fig.* 2).

When the engine is running at 3,000 r.p.m. the piston and connecting rod must go up the cylinder, stop, descend down the cyclinder and stop again (ready for the next ascent) fifty times every second and it is usual practice to counterbalance the crankshaft so that vibration is kept to a minimum.

Valve Mechanism
Most aero engines have **Overhead Valves,** that is to say, the valves are arranged to open and close in the top of the cylinder head. The valves, which resemble long-stemmed mushrooms, are kept closed by powerful **Valve Springs**. There is a tendency for valves to bounce as they snap shut and this is overcome by having two or perhaps three coil springs fitted one inside the other over the valve stem. As each spring has a different diameter their vibration characteristics cancel one another.

To achieve a good gas-tight fit the valves are ground and polished into their **Valve Seats**. When opened the inlet valve allows mixture to flow from the carburettor through the **Inlet Port** to the combustion chamber. Similarly the exhaust valve allows exhaust gases to flow from the cylinder through the **Exhaust Port** to the exhaust system. The stems of the valves slide in **Valve Guides** (*Fig.* 3).

It is essential that the valves open and close with a high degree of precision relative to the position of the piston and logically enough this is called **Timing**. When the crankshaft is in its uppermost position with the piston at the top of its travel the assembly is said to be at **Top Dead Centre** while the other extreme (piston at the bottom of its stroke) is called **Bottom Dead Centre**. Valve openings and closings are timed through suitable gearing to occur at a particular number of degrees before or after top or bottom dead centre according to the design of the engine. There is no need for the pilot to understand fully the complex design factors involved other than to mention that fuel/air mixture (or any gas) has inertia and with an engine running at high speed certain valve movements must be delayed to allow the gases to keep pace with the engine. For example the inlet valve remains open during the induction stroke for perhaps 10° after bottom dead centre so allowing the cylinder to become fully charged with mixture. Naturally the valve must close before the piston rises in the cylinder to any appreciable extent otherwise the mixture would be pumped back through the carburettor. Likewise at the end of the exhaust stroke the exhaust valve will remain open for say 10–15° after top dead centre to allow all the exhaust gases to escape. There may be a brief period when both inlet and exhaust valves remain open simultaneously (called **Valve Overlap**) but this is a design factor of little interest to the pilot. The valves are opened by rotating eccentric shafts called **Cams**. In aero engines it is usual for the cams to be situated within the crankcase, their movement being transmitted to the valve stems via **Pushrods** and **Rockers**. These components may be seen on most motor cycles (*Fig*. 3). The cams are accurately machined on a shaft there being a separate **Camshaft** for exhaust and inlet valves. The camshafts are geared to the crankshaft and run at half engine speed.

Ignition

Like valve timing the precise moment when the mixture is ignited is all-important. The spark has to be of sufficient intensity to ignite the petrol vapour and the sparking plug must provide the spark under conditions of high pressure and great heat. Width of spark is governed by the **Gap** between the **Central Electrode** of the plug and the **Side Electrode** (sometimes called the "earthed electrode"). *Fig*. 4 shows a typical sparking plug. High tension current for the spark is generated by a magneto on aero engines (an ignition coil is used in most cars) and provision is made for precise emission of the spark by a switching device (**Distributor**) operated by rotation of the magneto shaft. The device incorporates a pair of platinum **Points** which is adjusted to accurate limits to ensure that the spark occurs at the right time. It would be expected that ignition is timed to occur just after the piston has compressed the mixture and started to descend but it should be remembered that combustion in a piston engine is a progressive burning of the fuel which commences gradually, building up

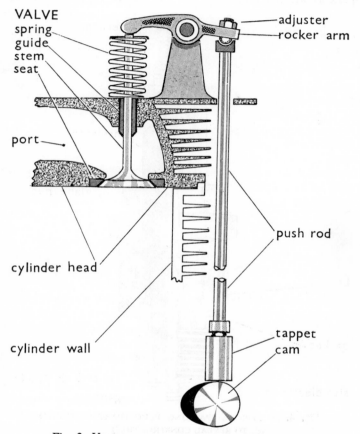

VALVE
spring
guide
stem
seat

adjuster
rocker arm

port

push rod

cylinder head

tappet
cam

cylinder wall

Fig. 3. VALVE AND ITS ASSOCIATED OPERATING
MECHANISM

as the flame spreads across the combustion chamber. Time is therefore required for full combustion to develop so that the spark is arranged to occur 10–15° before top dead centre

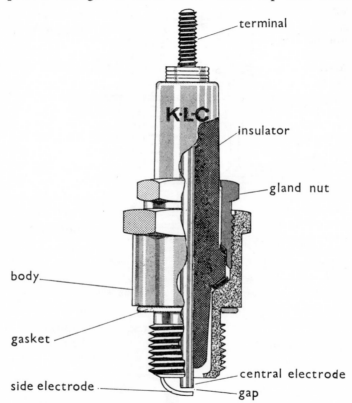

terminal

insulator

gland nut

body

gasket

side electrode

central electrode

gap

Fig. 4. A TYPICAL SPARKING PLUG (PART SECTIONED TO REVEAL CONSTRUCTION)

(BTDC). The higher the operating r.p.m. the more must the spark be **Advanced** (in cars it is the practice to fit an automatic advance/retard control which caters for various engine speeds and load conditions).

Lubrication

It is not generally realized that the balance between smooth running of an engine and irreparable damage is entirely dependent upon separation of the moving parts by a thin film of oil, often no more than one-thousandth of an inch in thickness. Dry metal-to-metal contact of fast moving parts is bound to result in the rapid build-up of heat through friction, to such an extent that within a matter of seconds the components would melt and **Seize** (fuse together).

Provision must therefore be made for a reservoir of lubricating oil of the correct **Viscosity** (thickness). It must not be so thick when cold that engine starting is made difficult yet it must be thick enough to provide adequate lubrication when it becomes thinned at engine running temperatures. An oil cooler is usually provided to prevent over-thinning of the oil. It may take the form of a separate oil radiator or the oil tank itself can be cooled by the airflow.

Whereas most cars are of **Wet Sump** design (i.e. oil is carried in a sump at the bottom of the crankcase) many aeroplanes have a separate oil tank and operate on the **Dry Sump** principle. In either case an engine-driven pump is provided to circulate oil under pressure through drillings in the engine which communicate with the main bearings, big-end bearings, cam-shaft bearings, valve rockers and other moving parts. Badly worn bearings allow the oil to seep out and cause a drop in oil pressure so that the oil pressure gauge is often a good indication of their condition. In addition to the pressure lubrication already mentioned certain parts such as the cylinder walls are **Splash Lubricated** as the crankshaft rotates and the big ends dip into the oil. After circulation oil may be returned to the sump by draining or **Scavenging** although many engines have a separate **Scavenge Pump** for the purpose. While performing its function oil collects minute particles of metal and carbon deposits so that **Filters** must be provided to keep it clean. These can be of the felt-element type which is replaced at regular intervals or there may be a permanent filter element which is cleaned by rotating a T-shaped handle on the filter casing.

Summing up lubrication, the oil has these vital tasks to perform in the engine—

1. Provision of a protective film which "plates" itself on moving parts so preventing metal-to-metal contact.
2. Dissipating heat generated by the moving parts.
3. Removal of impurities such as metal particles, carbon or other deposits which result from engine operation.
4. Provision of a gas-tight seal between valves and valve guides and piston rings and cylinder walls. To prevent oil working past the pistons and entering the combustion chamber a special **Oil Control** ring is fitted usually around the lower part of the piston skirt.

Cooling

Quite apart from the heat generated by fast moving parts is the very considerable heat resulting from combustion of the mixture. When running at 3,000 r.p.m. an engine such as the single-cylinder unit under discussion would ignite every two revolutions or

$$\frac{1,500}{60} = 25 \text{ times per second.}$$

Unless the surplus heat generated were dissipated in some way it would only be a matter of minutes before the cylinder head became red hot and the engine seized.

In a car the problem is solved by surrounding the cylinder and cylinder head with a series of passages cast in the cylinder block. Water pumped through these passages or **Water Jacket** is returned through a radiator and the heat dispersed by the air flowing through it. While **Liquid Cooling** has in the past been adopted for some very successful high performance aero engines (notably the Rolls-Royce Merlin) large engines are now practically confined to the gas turbine family. Lower powered aero engines have almost without exception always relied upon a cooling system which dispenses with the radiator and its tank, the water jacket around the cylinder and the coolant itself. This simpler and lighter method, in fact the one used on motor cycles and small petrol mowers, is called **Air**

Cooling. Fins are machined around the outside of the cylinder barrel and cylinder head and a system of sheet-metal **Baffles** guides the airflow through the engine cowling and around the fins carrying away the excess heat through the rear of the engine bay. Unfortunately some two-thirds of the fuel energy in an internal combustion engine is wasted, only the remaining third being converted to power.

All four-stroke engines, large or small, are based upon the simple unit described in the foregoing paragraphs. How these principles are applied to the specialized requirements of the aero engine is explained in the next section of this chapter, but before reading on the student is advised to study and understand fully the four-stroke cycle which is illustrated on page 14 (*Fig.* 5).

THE AEROPLANE ENGINE

So far the engine has been considered as a single-cylinder unit, producing, in the four-stroke design, one power stroke every two revolutions. Two cylinders arranged with a double crank so that one piston is at TDC while the other is at the bottom of its stroke will give a power stroke every revolution and a four-cylinder engine fires every half revolution. Power output from an engine is dependent upon the amount of force exerted by each piston during the power stroke multiplied by the number of times per minute the force is produced.

By definition time is an important factor of horse power. Remember one horse power is the amount of power required to raise 33,000 lb through a height of one foot in one minute. Equally one horse power is the equivalent of raising 66,000 lb through six inches in one minute or 330 lb through 50 ft in half a minute. In each case the amount of power is the same—33,000 ft/lb/min. It therefore follows that the engine designer may obtain the required power from his engine by

(*a*) using a number of small pistons and cylinders and running the engine at high speed,

(*b*) using fewer but larger pistons and cylinders at the same speed,

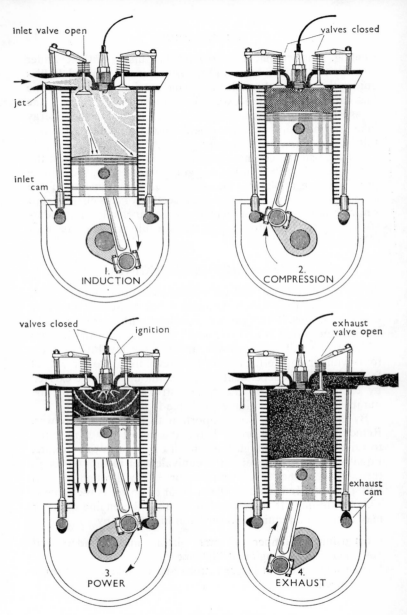

Fig. 5. THE FOUR-STROKE CYCLE

(*c*) reducing the speed of the engine and increasing the size of the pistons and cylinders.

Of course other measures can be taken to increase the power of an engine but these are often at the expense of long life and reliability, both essential requirements in an aero engine. While a six-cylinder engine is likely to be smoother running than a four-cylinder unit of the same power aero engines developing 150 h.p. or less are almost exclusively designed with four relatively large cylinders, the resultant engine being more robust than would be the case with six smaller piston/connecting rod assemblies.

The aeroplane engine differs from its automobile counterpart in a number of respects. Whereas the car engine is expected to operate under conditions of constantly changing speed and load, the aero engine has to run for long periods at a steady cruising power. High r.p.m., desirable in a car engine, are avoided in an aero engine because when rotational speeds exceed certain limits the tips or possibly a greater proportion of the propeller blades will exceed the speed of sound, creating shock waves which both dissipate engine power and reduce the all-important thrust required for flight. In consequence a high-revving aero engine requires some form of **Reduction Gear** between crank and propeller shaft and as this is a complication not favoured in the design of low-powered units the requirement of power at low r.p.m. can only be met by having a large engine. By way of illustration it is interesting to compare aero engines and car engines of similar power

	Humber Snipe	*Gipsy Major* I	3·8 *Jaguar*	*Lycoming* 0–S40
b.h.p.	137	130	220	250
Capacity cc	2,965	6,120	3,781	8,760
Maximum Power r.p.m.	5,000	2,350	5,500	2,575
No. of Cylinders	6	4	6	6

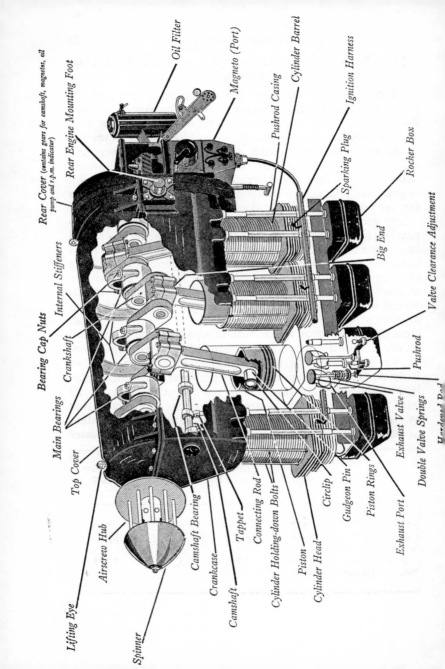

Oil Filter

Magneto (Port)

Rear Engine Mounting Foot

Rear Cover (contains gears for camshaft, magnetos, oil pump and r.p.m. indicator)

Pushrod Casing

Cylinder Barrel

Ignition Harness

Sparking Plug

Rocker Box

Valve Clearance Adjustment

Big End

Pushrod

Pushrod Rod

Exhaust Valve

Double Valve Springs

Exhaust Port

Piston Rings

Gudgeon Pin

Circlip

Cylinder Head

Piston

Cylinder Holding-down Bolts

Connecting Rod

Tappet

Camshaft

Camshaft Bearing

Crankcase

Spinner

Airscrew Hub

Lifting Eye

Top Cover

Main Bearings

Crankshaft

Internal Stiffeners

Bearing Cap Nuts

output. In each case it will be seen that power for power the aero engine is twice the size of the car engine but operates at approximately half the speed.

Arrangement of Cylinders

To some extent the design of the aeroplane engine is dictated by a need to arrange **Thrust** (i.e. propulsion from the engine(s)) in a suitable position relative to **Drag** (the total resistance of the wings, fuselage, etc. during flight) and although early engines had the cylinders fitted above the crankcase motor-car fashion it was soon realized that by inverting the engine a better thrust line would result accompanied by an improvement in the pilot's forward view over the nose of the aircraft. Until 1960 most of the lower-powered engines produced in Britain were of the **Inverted In-line** design, i.e. cylinders arranged in line below the crankcase. A classic example of this type of engine is the Gipsy Major in its various forms (*Fig.* 6) and the six cylinder Gipsy Queen.

In the U.S.A. engines in the low-power category have been developed on rather different lines with the cylinders placed horizontally on both sides of the crankcase. One of the advantages of the **Horizontally Opposed** engine is that it is shorter than an in-line unit of the same number of cylinders, the shorter crankshaft and crankcase resulting in an appreciable saving in weight (*Fig.* 7). As a measure of this aspect of efficiency an engine is said to weigh, for example, 1·98 lb/h.p. Although the horizontally opposed engine originated as a low-powered unit there now exists a very complete range starting from 35 h.p. and extending to eight-cylinder power plants (four each side of the crankcase) developing 400 h.p.

With the exception of a small number of Rolls-Royce "V twelve" liquid-cooled engines, higher-powered piston engines are now confined to the **Radial** design where the cylinders are spaced around a circular crankcase and the connecting rods are attached to a **Master Rod**, its bearing

Fig. 6. (*opposite*). GIPSY MAJOR I ENGINE

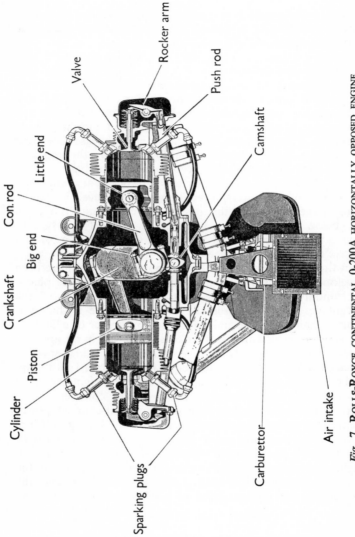

Cylinder

Piston

Crankshaft Con. rod

Big end

Little end

Valve

Rocker arm

Push rod

Camshaft

Sparking plugs

Carburettor

Air intake

Fig. 7. **Rolls-Royce** Continental 0-200A horizontally opposed engine

Illustration shows front pair of cylinders in section

running on a single crank within the crankcase. For power outputs in excess of 1,500 h.p. a second row of cylinders is placed behind the spaces between cylinders in the first row when the engine is designated a **Two Row Radial**. These various cylinder arrangements together with others no longer in current use are illustrated in *Fig.* 8.

Conversion of Power into Thrust

There would be no point in harnessing the engine to the wheels of an aircraft since once the machine left the ground propulsion would cease. Instead the engine is made to rotate a propeller or **Airscrew** which consists of two or more blades of airfoil section. Rather similar in action to a wood screw the propeller has its blades set at an angle to the plane of rotation, the angle being called **Pitch**. Because different parts of the blade move through the air at speeds which vary according to their distance from the centre of rotation (the tips being fastest) pitch is at its maximum where the blades join the propeller hub progressively reducing in angle towards the tip. In this way a constant angle relative to the airflow is achieved along the length of the blade. Propeller theory is complicated by the fact that blade angle relative to the air changes with forward speed and r.p.m. being at its maximum while the aircraft is at rest, reducing to a minimum during flight at maximum speed and assuming a negative angle in a steep dive. In consequence the propeller can only be at its most efficient during one condition of flight and the usual **Fixed Pitch** wood or metal airscrew is pitched for satisfactory cruising performance, a good propeller being 80–85 per cent efficient. Furthermore, the internal combustion engine develops power over a comparatively narrow range of r.p.m. and under certain conditions, particularly during the take-off and climb a propeller ideally suited to cruising flight may be too coarse in pitch to allow the engine to develop sufficient r.p.m. Under these circumstances the full power of the engine would not be available during the very moments of flight when most power is required so that, to some extent, the fixed-pitch propeller must compromise between providing a sufficiently coarse pitch for economical

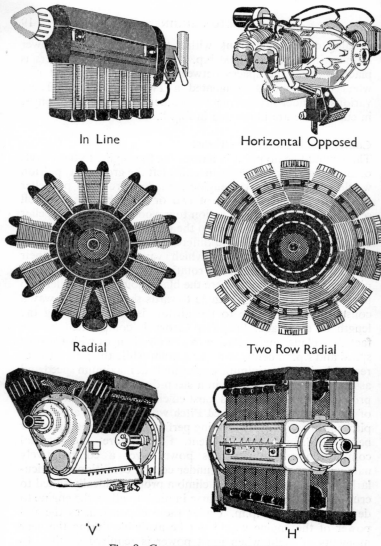

In Line

Horizontal Opposed

Radial

Two Row Radial

'V'

'H'

Fig. 8. CYLINDER ARRANGEMENTS

First four engines are air cooled, the lower two being liquid cooled. Very few 'V' engines remain in operation; the large 'H' engine with its two crankshafts has disappeared.

cruising flight, yet not so coarse that insufficient power is available to effect a good take-off and climb when speeds are low and the load on the propeller is high.

Although in the interest of economy and simplicity most light aircraft are fitted with fixed-pitch propellers their limitations will by now be clear and it is because of these limitations that more advanced aircraft are equipped with **Variable-pitch** airscrews which allow the pilot to select the most suitable pitch for each condition of flight. Usually the pilot exercises control through a **Constant-speed Unit** which automatically adjusts the blade angle according to the load on the propeller and the amount of throttle opening. The result of this arrangement is that the r.p.m. remain at the level set by the pilot on his **Pitch Control** irrespective of changes in load brought about by changes in air-speed (the r.p.m. on a fixed-pitch aircraft will increase during a dive at high air-speed and decrease in a low speed climb although the throttle is set in one position. This is because of the changing load on the propeller).

A constant-speed variable-pitch propeller may in many respects be likened to the automatic gearbox in a motor car.

Most light aircraft are fitted with two-bladed propellers but with bigger engines when more power has to be absorbed three, four or occasionally five blades are used.

Propellers are explained in greater detail in Chapter 2, Volume II of this series.

Auxiliary Services

Most aero engines are equipped with an electric starter and this, like its related component in a motor car, requires a heavy current for successful operation. An aircraft type accumulator must therefore be provided for engine starting and other purposes. So that it may be kept fully charged a generator is fitted to the engine. It is now becoming the practice to replace the generator with an alternator, its advantage being that a useful current occurs even at low engine speeds. This is particularly important during night flying when in addition to power required for the radio installation and navigation lights, taxi lights may be in use while manoeuvring on the ground at low throttle settings. To conserve the battery while on the ground it is usually possible to plug in a large capacity "trolley-acc" for starting and testing the various radio facilities prior to starting.

Most gyro instruments on the flight panel of a light aeroplane are vacuum operated although electric instruments are available. On multi-engined aircraft intended for two-pilot operation it is sometimes the practice to have one flight panel vacuum driven and the other electric so that two independent systems are provided as an insurance against failure.

While the required vacuum supply may be provided by a **Venturi Tube** situated outside the aircraft such an arrangement is dependent upon airflow and in consequence the gyro instruments will not function correctly until some minutes after take-off so delaying the pilot from entering cloud under condition of low ceiling until his instruments become operative. For serious instrument flying a vacuum pump is essential and this together with the generator or alternator is driven by the engine. Hydraulic services for undercarriage retraction and flap operation are often powered by an engine-driven pump.

Fuel tanks are sometimes situated in the wings of the aircraft or in a part of the fuselage that is some distance from the engine compartment and below the level of the carburettor. The engine-driven fuel pump is in the interest of safety duplicated by an electric pump.

Dual Ignition

With few exceptions even the most expensive motor cars run on one set of sparking plugs and a single ignition coil. For reasons of safety all aeroplane engines are required to have two separate ignition systems, i.e. two magnetos feeding two sets of sparking plugs through separate ignition leads. There is, however a less obvious reason for **Dual Ignition**. It will be remembered that the aeroplane engine is designed to develop its power at low r.p.m. Because of this design requirement it is invariably a large engine when related to power output so that large pistons and cylinders are used in conjunction with a combustion chamber of considerable volume.

While the large volume of compressed mixture could be
ignited by a single sparking plug, better combustion and
therefore more power results from having two sparking plugs
positioned one either side of the cylinder head. It is part of a
pilot's pre-flight checks to **Run up** the engine, testing each
ignition system in turn, and noting the decrease in r.p.m. or
Mag Drop as each switch is turned off. Conversely when the
switches are both in the ON position an increase in r.p.m. will
be seen on the engine-speed indicator thus demonstrating
that dual ignition increases power on a large slow-running
engine.

With the exception of a gradually decreasing number of
low-powered engines installed in simple light aeroplanes starting is performed electrically. Even so the engine is turned over
very slowly during starting and one of the following methods
has to be adopted to ensure that notwithstanding the slow
rotation of the magneto a high-intensity spark is provided for
starting—

1. **Booster Coil.** A battery-driven device similar to a car
   ignition coil which is pilot-controlled by a button during
   starting. The booster coil provides a spark until the
   engine is running under its own power when the magnetos
   are able to function and the booster button may be
   released.

2. **Impulse Starter.** A form of magneto which is driven by
   the engine via a spring. As the engine is turned over for
   starting, the spring, on becoming fully wound, flicks the
   magneto shaft at sufficient speed to generate a spark.
   To prevent "kick back" during starting the spark is
   retarded, ignition occurring after TDC. When the
   engine is running at some 700 r.p.m. bob-weights built
   into the impulse device fly outwards locking the spring
   drive in the correct position for advanced ignition.

3. **High-intensity Magneto.** The method favoured by most
   American manufacturers is to provide magnetos of large
   capacity which are capable of generating a spark at low
   rotational speeds.

Engine Handling

Dependent upon the complexity of the aircraft the engine is handled through some or all of the following controls—

1. Ignition switches
2. Fuel cock(s)
3. Throttle
4. Primer
5. Mixture control
6. Idle cut-off
7. Carburettor heat control
8. Fuel booster pump
9. Electric starter
10. Battery isolation switch
11. Propeller pitch control
12. Cooling gill control
13. Booster coil buttons
14. Supercharger control

The correct procedures to be adopted during starting, during various flight conditions and when stopping the engine are explained in the flying training manuals which form part of this series (Volumes I and II) and this chapter is concluded with a brief explanation of the engine controls listed above.

1. Ignition Switches. These may take the form of separate tumbler switches similar to the usual domestic light switch with the exception that in the DOWN position the ignition is off, the switches being UP for CONTACT. A separate switch is provided for each magneto and when hand starting only the switch controlling the impulse magneto (when fitted) should be used (*see* page 23). Alternatively the ignition may be controlled through a key-operated switch which has the following positions—

OFF
MAG 1
MAG 2
MAGS 1 and 2

With some installations the starter is engaged by turning the ignition key beyond the MAGS 1 and 2 position where it is held against spring pressure until the engine fires.

Whatever the type of switch when the ignition is in the OFF position the magnetos are earthed to the engine and so are unable to cause a spark.

2. Fuel Cock. Several fuel cocks may be provided in the aircraft fuel system or alternatively a single multi-position cock may handle fuel from whatever tank is selected by the pilot.

3. Throttle. This may be of the "plunger" or "lever" type. An adjustable friction device or **Throttle Nut** is often provided so that there is free movement of the throttle during taxi-ing and sufficient friction to hold the throttle in the position set by the pilot during cruising or other flight conditions.

In multi-engined aircraft a separate throttle is provided for each power unit.

4. Primer. When starting a cold engine a very rich mixture is required. In simple aeroplanes of older design it was the practice to "flood the carburettor" by depressing the float needle, when the resultant flow of petrol into the induction manifold provided the mixture required for starting. The primer is a small plunger-type pump which the pilot operates to inject petrol to the engine prior to cold starting. Care should be taken to ensure that the plunger is screwed home after use otherwise the mixture will be disturbed and rough running of the engine will result.

Most light aeroplane engines of American design may also be primed by pumping the throttle several times before starting. Rich mixture is in this case provided by an accelerator pump built into the carburettor for the main purpose of improving engine response to throttle opening.

5. Mixture Control. It was explained (page 3) that provision must be made to compensate for changes in air density which occur with changes in altitude. Without a mixture control to vary the fuel/air ratio the engine would run "rich" as the aircraft climbed into less dense air. This is a factor of some importance at heights in excess of 5,000 ft, materially affecting the economical operation of the aircraft. The mixture control is moved towards the WEAK position until there is a decrease in r.p.m. when it must be moved slightly in the opposite direction until the original engine speed is restored.

6. Idle Cut-off. Although it is possible to stop an engine by switching off the ignition, because of their design aeroplane engines have a tendency to "fire on" intermittently unless the throttle is opened wide as the propeller ceases to rotate. A cleaner stop will result when petrol is prevented from entering the slow-running jet and most aircraft have an idle cut-out for this purpose. It can take the form of a separate control or, more usually, it is brought into operation by moving the mixture control to the fully WEAK position.

Before operating the idle cut-out the engine should be allowed to run at 800–1,000 r.p.m. for a few moments, so enabling the engine to cool slowly to an even temperature. When the engine has been stopped the ignition switches *must* be put in the OFF position.

7. Carburettor Heat Control. Basically the carburettor is a device for atomizing fuel. This function is accompanied by a marked decrease in temperature within the area of the jets, due in part to the vaporization of petrol but also due to the decrease in pressure which occurs within the choke tube which, in turn, causes a drop in temperature (conversely while inflating a cycle tyre the pump becomes hot due to the rise in air pressure). When the outside air temperature is between 30°C and −18°C the cooling effect of the carburettor is sufficient to freeze the moisture content of the air when ice deposits will form on the butterfly valve and surrounding areas of the choke tube. The engine will slow down and eventually stop through carburettor icing.

To overcome this hazard ducting is arranged to convey air to the carburettor from two sources.

    1. Cold air from outside the aircraft.

2. Warm air from the environs of the engine bay. A two-way trap valve conveys hot or cold air to the carburettor according to the position of the carburettor heat control. The student may wonder why it is necessary to have this control when the cure for carburettor icing is simply a matter of drawing in warm air. While some light aircraft of older designs do in fact operate in warm air during cruising flight a linkage is nevertheless arranged so that on selecting take-off power the trap valve moves to the COLD AIR position. The piston engine relies for its power on the basic principle of expanding a mass of cold air by heating. It therefore follows that the more air available in the cylinders for expansion the greater will be the power developed by the engine. To a considerable extent this aspect of the piston engine (known as **Volumetric Efficiency**) is dictated by the density of the air entering the cylinder and since by pre-heating the air its density is reduced so a decrease in power will result when hot air is selected on the carburettor heat control. This drop in power may be demonstrated at any time by selecting hot air when the engine is running at or above cruising power.

Another method of dealing with the problem of carburettor icing is to replace the carburettor with a **Direct Injection** unit which introduces the correct quantity of atomized fuel via a separate injector nozzle position in each combustion chamber. Direct injection has the added advantage that very accurate metering of the fuel is attained and greater economy is therefore achieved than is possible with carburettor engines of the same power. To assist the pilot to attain best economy a fuel/air ratio meter may be included with the engine instruments.

8. Fuel Booster Pump. Because the fuel tanks are often below the level of the carburettor a pump must be included in the fuel system. Although engines are fitted with a diaphragm-type pump worked mechanically from the camshaft it is usual to have an additional electric pump, either immersed within the tank or similar in type to the usual car pump. As a safety precaution against failure of the engine-driven unit the booster pump must be switched on during take-off and landing or when engine failure may have resulted from malfunction of the engine-driven pump.

9. Electric Starter. Before the first engine start at the beginning of flying, after the switches have been checked and are OFF the engine should be turned over by hand

- (*a*) to free the engine from the effects of oil film adhesion and so reduce the load on the starter, and
- (*b*) to check that oil has not collected in the cylinders since severe damage would result should the engine start and one or more of the pistons come up against oil. Known as **Hydraulicing,** this condition, when it occurs, is usually confined to inverted engines or the lower cylinders of radials.

The starter should be operated for brief periods only, allowing time for battery recovery between each attempt to start the engine.

10. Battery Isolation Switch. This may take the form of a simple **Master Switch** which brings the battery into and out of circuit or when a "trolly-acc" socket is provided on the aircraft there will most likely be a **Ground–Flight** switch. In the GROUND position the internal battery is disconnected and the aircraft is dependent upon an external supply for starting, etc. After starting the switch is put in the FLIGHT position and the "trolly-acc" may then be removed leaving the aircraft to draw electricity from its own battery and generator.

11. Propeller Pitch Control. When, as is usually the case, a constant-speed unit is fitted the pilot exercises control of the propeller through the pitch control (usually adjacent to the throttle). Movement of this control alters the setting of a governor in the constant-speed unit so that engine speed is maintained at the level set by the pilot irrespective of aerodynamic load on the propeller or throttle setting, provided sufficient power has been set to speed the engine out of the idling range. Constant-speed units are illustrated on page 47 of Volume II in this series and their management in conjunction with throttle setting is explained in the accompanying text.

In multi-engined aircraft the propellers may be designed to **Feather**, i.e. the blades can be placed in a minimum drag, edge-on position so that a faulty engine may be prevented from rotation likely to cause further damage and drag is reduced to a minimum (Chapter 10, Volume II, explains Asymmetric Flight). Feathering is accomplished either by separate control or by moving the pitch levers to the FEATHER position.

Some propellers are designed to go into reverse pitch so that after landing power is used to create reversed thrust for shortening the landing run. A reverse thrust position is provided on the pitch control.

12. Cooling Gill Control. Usually only found on aircraft with engines of more than 250 h.p. the cooling gills control the flow of air through the engine cowling so enabling the pilot to maintain the engine(s) at their best working temperature.

13. Booster Coil Button. Particularly with large engines, rotation speeds during starting are low so that the magnetos are unable to generate a spark of good intensity. In extreme cases the spark may be too weak to start the engine and a separate ignition coil is required for use during starting. This is controlled by a booster coil button which must be pressed in until the engine is running on its magnetos.

14. Supercharger Control. The supercharger is a blower which may either be driven mechanically by the engine or through a turbine which is powered by exhaust gas. Its purpose is

  (*a*) to increase volumetric efficiency at altitude so that sea-level power is maintained at higher cruising levels, and
  (*b*) to boost engine power to above normal outputs during short periods when excess power is required (e.g. take-off, overshoot with flap and undercarriage extended, etc.).

Mechanically driven superchargers may be of the two-speed type which enable power to be maintained to considerable altitudes. The management of superchargers is dependent upon the type of installation but the student is unlikely to fly supercharged aircraft until conversion on to more advanced types.

CHAPTER 2

Meteorology

A KNOWLEDGE of the atmosphere, its properties and characteristics is as important to the pilot as a knowledge of the sea and its behaviour is to the sailor. Meteorology has been described as an "inexact science" no doubt because so many factors of an unpredictable nature are involved in forecasting. Nevertheless forecasting techniques continue to improve and in so far as the pilot is concerned an understanding of the subject is of immense value to the amateur and of prime importance to the professional.

THE ATMOSPHERE

The atmosphere is composed of a number of gases which for practical purposes can be called the air. It is however the properties of the air with which the pilot studying meteorology is chiefly concerned, principally temperature, pressure and humidity.

Temperature

A great deal of movement of air masses is a result of the effect of temperature. Heat from the sun causes air to rise and in turn air moves in to take the place of that which is displaced. Circulation of this kind may be local or it can extend over hundreds, even thousands of miles. Air which is heated in this way will continue to rise until it reaches an environment of similar temperature. Generally it may be considered that air temperature change with height is at a rate of 2°C per 1,000 ft and this is known as the **Lapse Rate.** It is a well-known fact that gases, when compressed, are heated (for example, a bicycle pump becomes hot while pumping). Conversely when gases are allowed to expand there is a temperature drop. The drop in temperature due to expansion, together with the lapse rate of 2°C/1,000 ft gives a total lapse rate (known as the **Dry Adiabatic Lapse Rate**) of 3°C/1,000 ft.

Humidity

The actual amount of humidity in any air mass is to a large extent dependent upon its origin. A mass travelling some thousands of miles mainly over the sea is known as a **Maritime** air mass while a mass conveyed over long tracts of land is known as a **Continental** air mass. Further, the origin of these air masses may give another clue to their characteristics, for example Polar Maritime, Polar Continental, Tropical Maritime and Tropical Continental.

When moist air rises it cools until it reaches its **Dew-point,** i.e. a temperature where any further cooling will cause condensation to take place. When this occurs latent heat is released which causes the temperature to drop at a lower rate. This **Saturated Adiabatic Lapse Rate** is approximately 1·5°C/1,000 ft.

Pressure

In meteorology pressure is measured in **Millibars**. By drawing lines on a chart joining places of equal pressure the weather picture emerges in much the same way as contour lines on a map will show the shape, formation and gradient of the land.

Atmospheric pressure is continually in a state of flux. Locally the changes may be small, but over a large area they can be considerable, particularly when intensely high (**Anticyclone**) or low (**Depression**) pressure weather systems are active. Naturally these pressure changes affect the altimeter and this aspect is dealt with later in the chapter.

CLOUDS
(Illustrated between pages 36 and 37.)

Throughout the text clouds are referred to by type name and the following list giving brief descriptions of each classification will help the student to understand the remainder of the chapter.

From this list it will be seen that clouds are classified into four main groups according to their height and appearance.

1. High Clouds. Heights above 20,000 ft. These clouds are often composed of ice crystals.

  (a) *Cirrus* (Ci): shapeless, wispy, white clouds. Sometimes referred to as "mares'-tails."

  (b) *Cirrocumulus* (Cc): has the appearance of ripples. White in colour and known as a "mackerel sky"; infrequently seen over the British Isles.

  (c) *Cirrostratus* (Cs): a thin, white veil-like cloud. Causes a halo to appear around the sun or the moon.

2. Medium Clouds. Heights between 7,000 ft and 20,000 ft.

  (a) *Altocumulus* (Ac): resembles patches of flattened globular masses sometimes arranged in waves or lanes.

  (b) *Altostratus* (As): layer of grey-blue cloud of fibrous appearance. May develop to considerable thickness.

3. Low Clouds. Heights near the ground.

  (a) *Stratus* (St): a dirty grey cloud lying close to the ground.

  (b) *Nimbostratus* (Ns): a thick dark rain-bearing cloud, often covering high ground. Ragged near rain-depositing areas.

  (c) *Stratocumulus* (Sc): a layer of patches or rolls of globular clouds, dark grey and light grey in colour. Flying conditions in and below these clouds are usually bumpy.

4. Heap Formed Clouds. Heights between 1,000 ft and 36,000 ft.

  (a) *Cumulus* (Cu): resemble large white smoke puffs. The entire sky may be dotted with these beautiful crisp clouds, and their formation is usually due to convection currents ascending on hot, sunny days. Base of cloud is always flat. Flying conditions may be turbulent, especially around midday.

(b) *Cumulonimbus* (Cb): a cloud of great vertical extent, often seen with well developed mushroom or anvil head which can extend up to 36,000 ft. Associated with electrical storms, but lightning is not particularly dangerous. Violent vertical air currents in and near these clouds can, however, be hazardous. Heavy icing is also a source of danger.

WIND

Wind is air in horizontal motion, caused generally by variations in atmospheric pressure over the earth's surface. Local winds or breezes, however, may be the result of uneven heating of an area, or they may be due to mechanical reasons, e.g. mountain ranges.

Veering and Backing
A wind is said to **Veer** when there is a clockwise change in direction. A **Backing** wind, on the other hand, changes direction anticlockwise.

Land and Sea Breezes
These are an example of local air movements. On a hot day, land near the sea is warmed more quickly than the neighbouring waters, the temperature of the air over the land is increased, the air expands, and rises, and cooler air from the sea flows in to take its place, setting up a gentle onshore breeze. At night the direction is reversed as the thermals die out over the cooling land and denser air is formed. This slowly spills out towards the sea (which is now warmer than the land) causing a light offshore breeze.

Surface Winds
At ground level winds encounter considerable resistance in the form of buildings, trees, hedges, hills, etc. These cause the wind velocity to fluctuate, and turbulent, gusty conditions become

stronger as the wind strength increases. This mechanical form of turbulence makes flying near the ground uncomfortably bumpy and can be dangerous to aircraft approaching to land when the air-speed is low. Landing over hangars or large buildings is never good practice but must be avoided on gusty days.

A fairly accurate means of estimating wind velocity at lower levels is that of observing cloud movements in relation to some fixed datum point, e.g. the corner of a hangar or wind-sock pole. When in the air, the path of cloud shadows over the ground is a useful aid in checking both wind speed and direction.

As a general rule, winds at heights in the region of 20,000 ft and above are westerlies. This means that easterly surface winds will decrease with altitude. Winds from the north must back to become westerly and southerly winds veer. The **Beaufort Scale** is used when reporting winds and for indicating wind speed and direction on weather maps (*Fig.* 9).

FOG

Fog is one of the airman's natural enemies and although modern techniques and equipment are being successfully developed to make automatic landings under such conditions a practical reality, these advantages will mainly apply to large commercial aircraft. A knowledge of the conditions under which fog is likely to form is invaluable to a practising pilot.

Radiation Fog

The ideal circumstances in which this type of fog will form occur where there is a moist air mass and the presence of temperature **Inversion** in the lower layers caused by rapid cooling of the ground so that the air nearest the ground is cooler than air above it. A layer of cloud will prevent heat radiating from the ground so that a clear sky is necessary for the formation of radiation fog. The consequent cooling causes the moist air (with a dew-point which is easily reached) to condense forming fog. The presence of microscopic nuclei suspended in the air (particularly in the lee of industrial areas) together with a light

Beaufort Number	Average Speed		Nearest related symbol	Descriptive Title	Observations
	m.p.h.	kt.			
0	0	0	◎	Calm	Smoke rises vertically
1	2	2		Light air	Direction shown by smoke but not wind sock
2	5	5		Light breeze	Wind felt on face; weather vanes revolve
3	10	9		Gentle breeze	Leaves and twigs in motion; wind sock is filled but limp; wind extends light flag
4	15	14		Moderate breeze	Small branches are disturbed; dust and loose papers raised
5	21	19		Fresh breeze	Small trees in leaf begin to sway
6	28	24	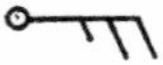	Strong breeze	Large branches in motion; telegraph wires whistle
7	35	30		Moderate gale	Trees in motion; inconvenience felt when walking against wind
8	42	37	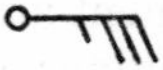	Fresh gale	Breaks twigs off trees; walking made difficult
9	50	44	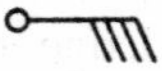	Strong gale	Slight structural damage occurs; chimney pots and slates removed
10	59	52	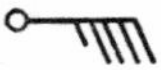	Whole gale	Trees uprooted; considerable damage occurs
11	69	60		Storm	Rarely experienced; very widespread damage
12	Above 75	Above 65		Hurricane	
				Wind direction reported but not speed	

Fig. 9. THE BEAUFORT SCALE OF WIND FORCES AND ASSOCIATED WEATHER CHART SYMBOLS

PLATE 1

Clouds of the warm front—cirrus and cirrostratus

A line of tufted cirrus marks the upper limits of an approaching warm front. Merging into the cirrus is cirrostratus with altostratus at a lower level still. The base of the incline and actual ground front is some 600 miles away.

36

PLATE 2

Cirrus in typical plumed formation
(Courtesy of the Royal Meteorological Society)

Cirrus, cirrocumulus, and cirrostratus in bands
(Courtesy of the Royal Meteorological Society)

PLATE 3

Cirrostratus showing halo effect
(Courtesy of the Royal Meteorological Society)

Altocumulus (banded formation)
(Courtesy of the Royal Meteorological Society)

PLATE 4

Altostratus obscuring the sun
(Courtesy of the Royal Meteorological Society)

Stratus shrouding the hill-tops
(Courtesy of the Royal Meteorological Society)

PLATE 5

Nimbostratus low over the roof-tops
(Courtesy of the Royal Meteorological Society)

Stratocumulus
(Courtesy of the Royal Meteorological Society)

PLATE 6

Cumulus developing into cumulonimbus (*below*)
(Courtesy of the Royal Meteorological Society)

Cumulonimbus with anvil developing
(Courtesy of the Royal Meteorological Society)

PLATE 7

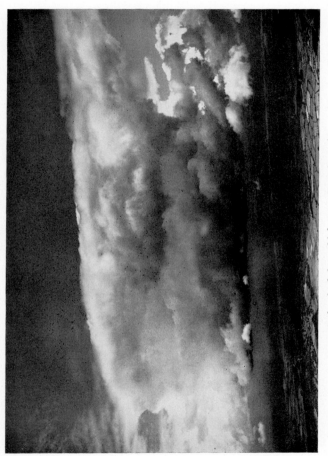

A cloud of the cold front—Cumulonimbus

The anvil-shaped head, well defined in this photograph, together with the associated showers or thunderstorms, are the chief characteristics of the cumulonimbus cloud. Turbulence within these clouds is of greater danger to aircraft than lightning.

(Courtesy of *Flight*)

PLATE 8

Cumulonimbus showing well developed anvil
(Courtesy of the Royal Meteorological Society)

Fair-weather cumulus
(Courtesy of the Royal Meteorological Society)

wind to complete the mixing of the nuclei and moisture would assist the process and increase the vertical extent of the fog.

Hill Fog
Is simply low cloud which envelops the ground and reduces the visibility to less than 1,100 yd, the datum where fog is deemed to exist.

Sea Fog
This is associated with coastal areas where relatively moist air is cooled to below its dew-point, the resultant condensation forming fog which can move over coastal areas. It is the movement of moist air in contact with a cold surface that makes the sudden appearance or "drifting in" of this type of fog a hazard.

Advection Fog
Similar to sea fog its formation is a result of movement of air over a cooler surface. Although not so frequent in the United Kingdom it can appear unexpectedly, for example, when mild weather follows a severe cold spell, a typical example being a thaw.

The formation of fog is dependent upon the **Relative Humidity** of the air, i.e. the amount of invisible water vapour present in a volume of air compared with the maximum amount of water vapour it could hold at that temperature before becoming saturated (when the water vapour would then become visible). Thus 50 per cent relative humidity means that the air is half saturated; 100 per cent fully saturated. From this information may be found the **Dew-point**, i.e. the temperature at which the air becomes saturated. For example an air mass may be measured to be, say, 8°C above its dew-point. Should the temperature drop by 8°C the air will become saturated and fog will occur. From this it will be seen that warm air is able to contain more water vapour than cold and indeed fog is dispersed when the air is heated from above by the sun. It is also readily dispersed by wind.

Whenever there is a risk of fog careful flight planning is essential with regard to fuel reserves and diversion airfields.

PRECIPITATION

Rain

Cloud is made up of water droplets, normally only one-hundredth of a millimetre in diameter, which fall relative to the surrounding air at a rate of six inches or so per minute. Possibly owing to a process of attraction these particles collide with one another during their descent through the cloud, amalgamating to form larger drops which may grow in diameter to 5·5 mm or beyond although when subjected to powerful currents these larger drops tend to break up into 5·5 mm units which may be regarded as maximum size raindrops. As the droplets grow in size so their descent velocity increases until they are able to overcome the ascending air currents within the cloud and drop to earth in the form of rain. As a general rule the greater the vertical extent of cloud the bigger the raindrop so that layer type clouds produce light rain or drizzle while heap or cumulus types cause heavy rain.

Hail

It has been calculated that an up-current of some 1,600 ft/min is required to support a maximum size raindrop. In large cumulonimbus clouds these speeds will very likely be exceeded many times. These vertical currents tend to fluctuate so that the falling raindrop may be arrested, carried up to the freezing levels of the cloud and dropped several times, on each occasion collecting a further layer of glazed or rime ice until the hail is of sufficient weight to drop free of the cloud. Given the facilities it is possible to cut open a hailstone and count the various layers it has collected while journeying up and down within the cloud. Although hailstones in the U.K. rarely grow to dangerous proportions, in certain parts of Africa examples have been recorded weighing up to 2 lb and having a diameter of four or even five inches. Clearly large hailstones are capable of causing very considerable damage to buildings and aircraft encountering them in flight. Since heavy hailstones are associated with the largest cumulonimbus clouds and violent thunderstorms, these should be avoided, particularly in parts of the world where such hailstones are by no means uncommon.

Snow and Sleet

Although cloud will remain composed of water droplets at temperatures well below freezing (**super-cooled**) higher cloud regions beyond 20,000 ft or so take the form of ice crystals. However, when the ground temperature drops by more than a few degrees below freezing precipitation is bound to be in the form of snowflakes. A close examination under a microscope reveals these to be composed of ice crystals formed in a variety of intricate and beautiful patterns of perfect symmetry, usually arranged in a basic hexagonal design. Large moist ice crystals readily amalgamate to form these snowflakes which will retain their crispness while falling to the ground unless the layers of air beneath the cloud are warm enough partly to melt the crystals when sleet will occur. Sleet may also be a combination of snow and rain.

Unlike super-cooled water droplets, snowflakes being frozen and of very little density present no hazard to flight other than a reduction in visibility which may be considerable. Snowflakes do not adhere to the airframe.

FRONTAL SYSTEMS AND THE FORMATION OF A DEPRESSION

The Norwegian meteorologist, Professor Bjerkens is responsible for the now widely accepted theory of the birth of a depression. This concludes that a warm and a cold air mass moving adjacent to one another will cause a decrease in pressure accompanied by the intrusion into the colder air of a wedge of warmer air. The warm and colder air masses may be moving in opposite directions to one another or in similar directions but at different speeds so that a relative motion exists between them. Various stages in the formation of a depression are shown in *Fig*. 10. The divisions between the wedge of warm air and the surrounding colder atmosphere are called **Fronts**. It should be understood that the difference between the two air masses either side of the fronts may only be that of a few degrees in temperature and small changes in pressure and/or humidity characteristics.

Low-pressure systems are usually associated with bad weather and a deep depression is almost certain to bring low cloud and rain. The path of these "lows" across the British Isles is usually easterly at a rate of approximately 20 kt.

On a weather map or **Synoptic Chart** a low-pressure system is shown as a series of concentric **Isobars**, i.e. lines along which the mean sea level (m.s.l.) pressure is of equal value—the closer the isobars the greater will be the change in pressure over that area. It is this **Pressure Gradient** which determines the strength of the wind.

Because a fluid will always flow from an area of high pressure to one that is lower it would perhaps be expected that in a low-pressure system, the surrounding relatively high-pressure atmosphere would flow in towards the centre. However, as a result of the rotation of the earth in the northern hemisphere wind at ground level circulates around a depression in an anti-clockwise direction, blowing in towards the centre at an angle of approximately 30° to the isobars (*Fig*. 11), the direction of rotation being reversed south of the equator. At ground level the wind is retarded because of friction caused by hills, trees, buildings, etc. As friction decreases with height so the wind speed increases until at approximately 1,500 ft above ground level the forces resulting from the earth's rotation and the low-pressure system become stabilized and the wind blows parallel to the isobars. This is known as the **Geostrophic** wind (*Fig*. 12).

Secondary Depression
This is a smaller low within the main system. Its path around the primary depression is in an anticlockwise direction. Gales and thunderstorms are often caused by these conditions (*Fig*. 13).

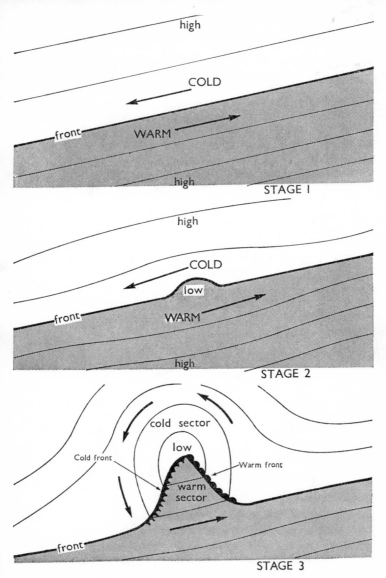

Fig. 10. FORMATION OF A DEPRESSION

Stage 1: Front separating cold and warm air masses.
Stage 2: Intrusion of warm air into cold region.
Stage 3: Depression fully developed.

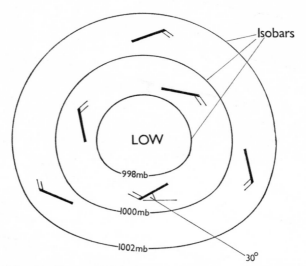

Fig. 11. FLOW OF SURFACE WINDS AROUND A DEPRESSION

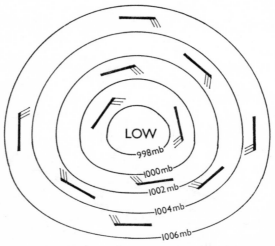

Fig. 12. FLOW OF UPPER WIND AROUND A DEPRESSION

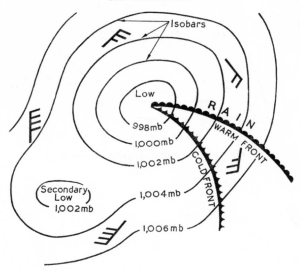

Fig. 13. SECONDARY DEPRESSION

Trough of Low Pressure

A trough generally forms in the shape of a U or V. The region of lowest pressure found at the centre of the trough gives rise to poor flying conditions (*Fig.* 14).

Anticyclone or High

Anticyclones are associated with fair or fine weather and usually move quite slowly across the country, often becoming stationary for several days. *Fig.* 15 shows how a high appears on a synoptic chart. The arrows indicate light winds circulating in a clockwise direction and deflected outwards at ground level. At 1,500 ft the direction of the wind is along the isobars (in the southern hemisphere winds flow round a high in an anticlockwise direction).

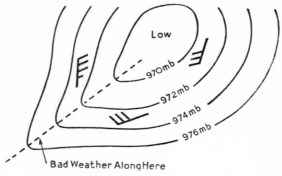

Fig. 14. TROUGH OF LOW PRESSURE

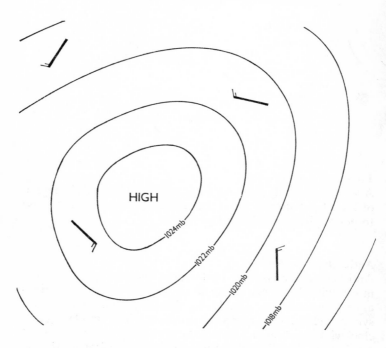

Fig. 15. HIGH PRESSURE SYSTEM SHOWING WIND FLOW
AT GROUND LEVEL

Upper winds circulate in a direction parallel to the
isobars

Ridge of High Pressure

Fine weather of from twelve to twenty-four hours' duration followed by worsening conditions often marks the passing of a ridge of high pressure.

Col

A region between two lows and two highs is known as a col.

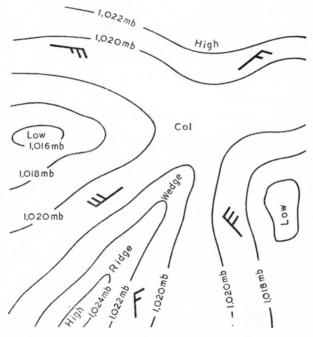

Fig. 16. A COL FORMED BETWEEN TWO LOW AND HIGH PRESSURE REGIONS

Weather conditions in this system are likely to be unstable and may last from twelve to twenty-four hours (*Fig*. 16).

Fronts

It is not uncommon to hear radio announcers state that warmer air is approaching from the south-west, or perhaps a rain belt is expected to pass south-eastwards across the country. Such predictions of changes in weather are often the result of observations made by weather ships or outlying stations. Using scientific instruments meteorologists are able to plot the advance of particular types of air masses and pressure systems. The dividing band between two adjacent air masses is often many miles wide and while the contrast between conditions in each mass may only be slight, occasionally the change in weather is very sudden, and the unwary pilot may find himself far from home under deteriorating weather conditions.

The Warm Front

When describing the formation of a depression (page 39) it was explained how a mass of warm, moist air forms a wedge-shaped intrusion into an adjacent belt of colder air. This wedge is known as the **Warm Sector** of the depression and from time to time weather systems of this kind move in from the south-west Atlantic and drift across the British Isles. When the warm sector encounters colder and denser air it rises on a shallow incline of approximately 1 in 125. The ascending air cools and because it is moist, cloud is formed. The extreme edge of the advancing warm air can rise to a height of 30,000 ft or more, creating a line of cirrus cloud. To an observer on the ground cirrus presents a clear indication that a warm front is approaching. As the front moves over the observer the cirrus cloud will be followed by cirrostratus descending and thickening into altostratus until finally, reaching almost down to ground level will come thick, rain-bearing nimbostratus. Heavy rain from this cloud is likely to extend 200 miles ahead of the actual ground front and the leading edge of cirrus cloud may be 600 miles ahead of where the warm front ends at near ground level. With the passing of the warm front rain ceases and as the warm sector arrived over the observer he would notice a rise in temperature, a change in wind direction (veer) and the barometer,

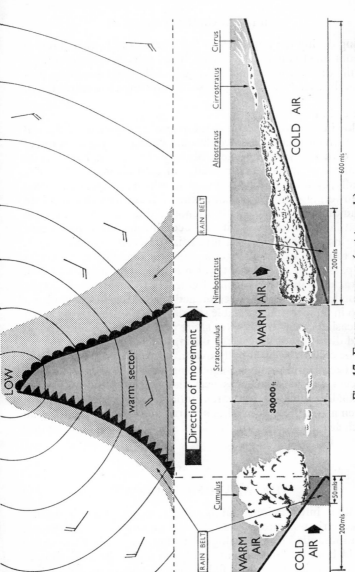

Fig. 17. FRONTAL SYSTEMS (not to scale)

Lower portion of illustration shows warm and cold fronts as seen from ground level while upper section of the drawing shows the same frontal systems in plan.

falling during the approach of the front, would either stabilize or continue to fall at a greatly reduced rate. Flying conditions within the warm section usually include poor visibility and some drizzle. *Fig*. 17 shows a section through the warm front.

The Cold Front
Following the warm sector in a low-pressure system is a second front which occurs when colder and denser air intrudes under the relatively warmer content of the warm sector. The warmer air ahead of the advancing wedge of cold air is forced to rise rapidly, creating unstable conditions which are usually marked by towering cumulus cloud. Some of these may develop into cumulonimbus clouds with attendant thunderstorms and the usual dangers associated with these conditions. Severe turbulence is the main hazard with lightning being of secondary importance.

A rain belt extending over a depth of some fifty miles marks the passage of a cold front which is usually of a more broken character than a warm front. Returning to the observer on the ground, after the warm sector had passed he would notice a drop in temperature, possible squalls with the mean wind speed increasing considerably over short periods and a sharp veer in wind direction of up to 180° during the squall (*Fig*. 17).

The cold front eventually overtakes the warm front and the two become intermingled squeezing out the warm sector in a process which commences near the centre of the depression gradually extending outwards until no warm sector remains. When a cold front overtakes a warm they combine to form an **Occluded Front** and the various stages of development are shown in *Fig*. 18.

THE WEATHER FORECAST

Weather information, that is to say, temperature, humidity, barometric pressure, cloud type and amount, etc., is collected by thousands of meteorological stations situated all over the world both on land and at sea. In so far as the U.K. is concerned this information is fed through a teleprinter network to

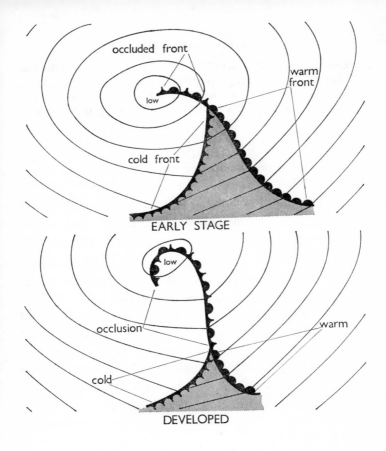

occluded front

warm front

low

cold front

EARLY STAGE

low

occlusion

warm

cold

DEVELOPED

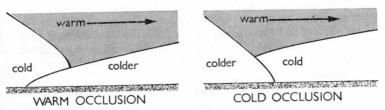

warm →

cold   colder

WARM OCCLUSION

warm →

colder   cold

COLD OCCLUSION

Fig. 18. FORMATION OF OCCLUSION

Type of occlusion (bottom drawings) is dependent upon relative temperatures of the two cold air masses.

the Central Meteorological Office and then circulated to the outlying stations. The reports are conveyed by an international numerical code; data from each station take the form of three groups of numbers which relate to the following headings—

$$111 \; C_L \; C_M \qquad ww \; VhN_h \qquad DD \; F \; W \; N$$

111	Identification number of the weather station	(Three figures)
C_L	Type(s) of low cloud	(Single figure)
C_M	Type(s) of medium cloud.	(Single figure)
ww	Weather at time of report	(Two figures)
V	Visibility	(Single figure)
h	Height of base of low cloud	(Single figure)
N_h	Amount of low cloud under previous heading	(Single figure)
DD	Surface wind direction	(Two figures)
F	Beaufort scale wind force (*see* page 36)	(Single figure)
W	Past weather	(Single figure)
N	Total amount of cloud of all types in the sky	(Single figure)

The position of each reporting station is marked on special weather maps and when the coded information has been translated by the receiving office it is added in symbol form around the reporting station to which it refers. The positioning of the symbols around the station marked on the weather map is in standard form and the complete unit is called the **Station Model** (*Fig.* 19). A comprehensive list of symbols is shown in Appendix 2.

When all the station models have been completed on the weather map the forecaster will draw in isobars joining places of equal barometric pressure (page 40). From the completed

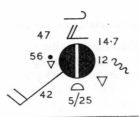

Example Plotted	Met. Element Represented	Meaning of Example
☀ ‿‿⌐	Type of high cloud	Cirrus
⫽	Type of medium cloud	Altostratus
14·7	Pressure reduced to m.s.l.	1,014·7 mb
☀ 12	Barometric tendency	Barometer has fallen 1·2 mb since previous reading
☀ ⌇	Barometric tendency	Falling unsteadily
☀ ▽	Past weather	Showers
⌒	Type of low cloud	Cumulus
5/25	Amount and height of low cloud	Five-eighths of sky covered at 2,500 ft
☀ 42	Dew-point temperature	42°F
╱	Wind-speed and direction	215°/13–18 m.p.h.
•̇▽	Present weather	Rain showers, slight
☀ 56	Visibility	6 kilometres
47	Temperature	47°F
◖	Circle indicates position of reporting station: total cloud amount plotted within circle, e.g. ⅞	

* Entered in red.

Fig. 19. THE STATION MODEL

Table below the station model explains the meaning of each symbol. A complete list of symbols is shown in Appendix 2.

synoptic chart the weather prevailing at each reporting station can be recognized. Furthermore by comparing the current chart with one drawn several hours previously a weather tendency will emerge with sufficient clarity to enable a forecast to be made. An example of a synoptic chart is shown in *Fig*. 20.

District Forecasts
For meteorological purposes the British Isles and surrounding seas are divided into a number of areas of approximately equal size. Based upon the general inference local geographical features are taken into account to arrive at a detailed forecast within each area.

Local Forecasts
These cover a much more confined area and a local forecaster, having accumulated experience at his centre, is able to anticipate with reasonable accuracy the effect of approaching fronts or pressure systems. Because of his knowledge of local conditions he is in the best position to forecast local winds, fog risk or rain, etc.

Route Forecasts
As the name implies this is a special type of forecast intended to cover a particular route. Because the rapidity of a forecasted weather change is often the most difficult factor to anticipate it follows that the shorter the route the more accurate the forecast is likely to be. Route forecasts may be amended by radio during flight from data often originating from other aircraft.

Special Forecasts
Most large civil and military aerodromes have a forecasting centre where forecasts may be obtained either for a specific route or for a local area.

It is good practice to develop "weather appreciation" by studying local conditions (wind direction, temperature, appearance of the sky, etc.) and comparing this assessment with the official forecast. As experience increases accuracy will improve.

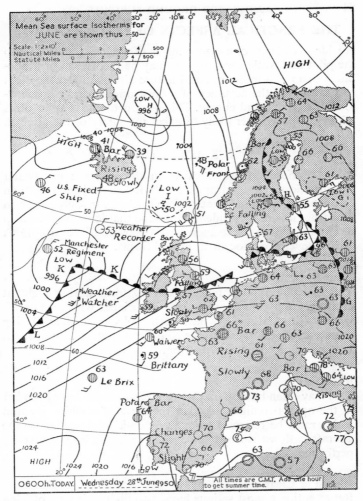

Fig. 20. A SYNOPTIC CHART
(By permission of the Controller of H.M.S.O.)
Because of the small scale this illustration is simplified.

THE PRACTICAL ASPECTS OF METEOROLOGY

A wide knowledge of meteorology is of obvious importance to
the pilot and while some aspects may be theoretical or acade-
mic, others of a more practical nature directly affect the flight
of the aircraft, the accuracy of its instruments and the behaviour of airframe and engine. This section of the chapter deals
with types of weather likely to affect the safety of the aircraft.

ICE ACCRETION

In the atmosphere water exists in three forms: gas (water
vapour), liquid (water droplets) and solid states (ice). It is often
erroneously supposed that airframe icing can only occur in
cloud but it is more prudent to assume that icing may develop
at any time when the temperature is between $0°C$ and $-40°C$.
Airframe icing can occur in several forms.

Hoar Frost

This is commonplace but unlikely to form during flight at
cruising level. It is more usually associated with an aircraft
when its external surfaces have been cooled at altitude. During
a descent, should the airframe come into contact with warmer,
moist air hoar frost may develop.

Rime Ice

This may often be seen on cars or aircraft which have been left
in the open overnight. It takes the form of a white, icy film
which must be removed (usually by de-icing fluid) before the
aircraft is flown since rime ice may seriously impair take-off
performance.

Glazed or Clear Ice

Representing a most serious hazard to flight this type of icing
may build up very rapidly, materially altering the contours of
the leading portions of the wing with attendant aerodynamic
deterioration (*Fig.* 21). When icing of this kind is severe it is
important to change flight level by climbing or descending out

of the icing temperature range (with due regard to safety heights and air traffic considerations). Aircraft experiencing such conditions while flying on airways invariably request control to allow a change in flight level.

Principal Cause of Glazed Ice

It is common knowledge that at temperatures below freezing water turns into ice but in the atmosphere very pure water can remain fluid in the form of super-cooled water droplets although their temperature is below 0°C. On impact with an aircraft their state is changed and the super-cooled droplets smear and freeze on to the contacting surface. The rate of build-up is dependent upon the amount and size of water droplets, their temperature, etc. Severity of icing to be expected during flight will be given on the forecast as an **Icing Index** and may be listed as "slight," "moderate" or "severe" although the distinction between these terms has not been clearly defined. However it is the responsibility of the pilot to be aware of the conditions under which icing can occur. The forecast will include a **Freezing Level** which will change when passing through a frontal system (*Fig.* 22).

Because of its detrimental effect on the aerodynamic efficiency of the wing, icing will raise the stalling speed, reduce the effectiveness of the controls and decrease the airspeed while at the same time increasing the weight of the aircraft. Modern **De-icing** and **Anti-icing** equipment may operate by thermal or mechanical means and has done much to eliminate this hazard. There is, however, the additional problem of keeping aerials, insulators and antennae free of ice, usually with a special paste. The pitot head is electrically heated.

In addition to airframe icing there are also engine considerations. For example a build-up of ice in the air intake will reduce the volume of air reaching the power unit and in piston engines the mixture will be seriously disturbed. Ice will readily form within the carburettor even when the outside air temperature is well above freezing (page 26).

Ice guards, heated intakes and hot air ducting have made these problems less formidable than they were but the pilot

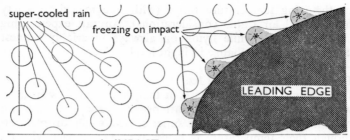

1. IMPACT

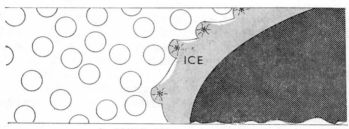

2. BUILD-UP

3. TURBULENT AIRFLOW

Fig. 21. THE FORMATION OF GLAZED ICE

1. Impact of super-cooled water on leading edge. Note smearing of water droplets.
2. Build-up of irregular layer of ice.
3. Breakdown of airflow.

must nevertheless be aware of the possible dangers and fully understand the operation of the carburettor heat control.

Propellers are by no means immune from icing which may cause vibration. Although usually of little consequence ice shedding from propellers on multi-engined aircraft will often cause

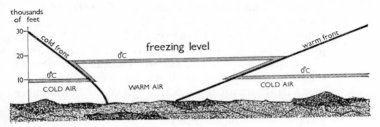

Fig. 22. CHANGES IN FREEZING LEVEL IN FRONTAL SYSTEM

unexpected and alarming noises as it strikes the fuselage. Aircraft intended for regular operation in icing conditions are equipped with propeller de-icing equipment.

TURBULENCE

Normally the greatest source of turbulence is found in cloud, the most severe being associated with cumulonimbus. Moderate turbulence presents no particular problem, but under the most extreme conditions special considerations apply. Within cumulonimbus clouds vertical currents in excess of 4,000 ft/min may be experienced creating forces of such magnitude as to impose great stresses on the airframe. Rapid changes in altitude and attitude call for an appreciation of the factors involved and the pilot must resist the temptation to struggle with the controls since this will only add to the stresses already set up by turbulence. Changes in relative airflow brought about by the vertical currents will likewise alter the angle of attack and when this is coupled to an increase in *g* loading stalling speed will be very much above normal. To reduce the risk of structural damage when flying through severe turbulence the pilot should

(a) Ignore the wildly fluctuating Air-speed Indicator and Altimeter and concentrate on maintaining lateral and fore and aft level (Artificial Horizon and Turn and Slip Indicator) and heading (Direction Indicator).

(b) Reduce power setting to a level known to produce a cruising speed some 15 per cent below normal, this representing a good compromise between adequate margin above stalling speed and the slowest speed possible to relieve stresses resulting from turbulence. (*Note*. In many light aircraft the A.S.I. is marked with an amber cautionary sector which must be avoided when flying through severe turbulence.)

Although clouds are the principal source of turbulence under certain conditions land features will create disturbances of which the downdraught is an example. Downdraughts can be very severe particularly on the leeward side of hills, a fact which should always be borne in mind when airfields are situated near features likely to cause air disturbances of this kind.

The behaviour of wind near uneven ground may be demonstrated by watching a fast flowing stream as it makes its way over a rock-strewn bed. To overcome a stone the water must rise in a small wave and then descend leaving behind an area of foam and eddies. If the obstacle is large enough the flow may even reverse, encouraging flotsam to float upstream. Air in motion near the ground will behave in a very similar manner. In addition to the horizontal flow there are up-currents, down-currents, eddies and gusts all of which contribute to a fluctuation in surface wind velocity. Hills, ridges and even large buildings all create ground turbulence and both the windward and leeward sides of such obstacles may present a danger, particularly to low-powered light aircraft. *Fig*. 23 shows the flow of air over a high ridge and the path of an aircraft attempting to fly overhead. The pilot approaches the summit with what he considers to be a safe margin of height. On entering the area of downdraught a descent begins and if the aircraft is low-powered the pilot may be unable to maintain height or have sufficient speed or room to turn away from the danger.

It is therefore important to clear ridges and hills by a margin of several hundred feet, particularly during conditions of strong wind.

During summer lines of small cotton-wool-like cumulus clouds (sometimes called **Fair Weather Cumulus**) will indicate

Fig. 23. THE DANGERS OF A DOWN-CURRENT IN LEE OF A HILL

the existence of thermal or warm air currents which are the result of uneven heating of the ground. For example, air flowing over sand dunes, large buildings or asphalt areas will take on a higher temperature than air standing over fields or lakes. Air warmed by these hotter areas will rise, its place being taken by a current of colder air from surrounding regions and a thermal circulation will develop.

Occasionally thermal turbulence can be very active causing flying at lower altitudes to be most unpleasant. Rare cases have been reported where bumpiness from one cause or another has been so violent that the occupants of aircraft have been thrown from their seats, sustaining injuries as a result. The moral is clear. When flying through turbulent conditions of any kind, reduce air-speed and be sure that the passengers are strapped in securely.

THUNDERSTORMS

At one time flying in or through thunderstorms was considered to be foolhardy but with the development of aircraft and radio aids to navigation flight in thunderstorms is now regarded as merely unpleasant and to be avoided wherever possible. **Weather Radar** is carried in the nose of many transport aircraft so that particularly large cumulonimbus clouds may be detected well ahead and, in the interest of passenger comfort, avoided but there are times when for flight planning, air traffic or other reasons it is necessary to fly through thunderstorms.

The problems associated with turbulence and icing have already been mentioned. It is also not uncommon to experience a good deal of hail when entering the storm. Lightning itself, although distracting, is not of very great importance and even a lightning strike may do little other than affect the compass, interfere with radio reception and produce a smell of ozone. All components of the aircraft are **Bonded**, i.e. connected together in electrical continuity so that during a thunderstorm, electrical discharge is able to spread evenly without "flashover" between components, thus preventing serious damage to the aircraft or harmful effects to the occupants. Circumstances permitting, the worst turbulence can often be avoided by penetrating the storm at flight levels below 10,000 ft.

When flight through a thunderstorm is imminent and unavoidable the pilot should take the following actions—

Before Entry
1. Instruct the passengers to fasten their seat belts securely.
2. Secure all loose articles.
3. Disengage the auto pilot.
4. Turn up the cockpit lighting to its maximum brightness This will prevent temporary blindness as a result of lightning flashes.
5. Switch off all radio equipment rendered inoperative by static interference from the storm.
6. Operate the anti-icing and de-icing equipment, not forgetting to check that the pitot heater is switched on.

7. Reduce power to the recommended setting for flight within turbulence and re-trim to hold the lower air-speed that will result.
8. Check the vacuum and/or electric supply to the instruments.
9. Before entering the storm synchronize the direction indicator with the magnetic compass.

After Entry
1. Concentrate on controlling the aircraft with special reference to lateral and fore and aft level (Artificial Horizon). Avoid any control movements likely to add to the severe airframe stresses set up by the storm.
2. Unless there is risk of hitting an obstacle ignore the fluctuating readings of the altimeter and the air-speed indicator.
3. Do not attempt to turn other than for small heading corrections.
4. When weather radar is fitted it will indicate the best way through the storm but in the absence of this aid it is usually best to keep flying straight ahead.

After flying through a bad electric storm the magnetic compass may be affected and a compass swing may be necessary.

From the foregoing it will be apparent that only fully equipped aircraft should be flown through cumulonimbus cloud and pilots of light aircraft should whenever possible keep well clear of these clouds, particularly during thundery conditions.

THE ALTIMETER

The average mean sea level barometric pressure is regarded as 14·7 lb/sq in., (1,013·2 mb), i.e. the weight of air bearing on each square inch of surface area. A mountain top 10,000 ft above sea level is subjected to a column of air 10,000 ft shorter than one reaching down to sea level and being shorter it will naturally exert less pressure than the sea level value of 14·7 lb/

sq in. It therefore follows that atmospheric pressure decreases with gain in height above sea level and upon this fact is founded the concept of the pressure altimeter. Basically the altimeter is a very sensitive aneroid barometer with a dial calibrated in feet instead of pressure units. The instrument is calibrated to International Standard Atmospheric conditions which assume a sea-level pressure of 1013·2 mb, a sea-level temperature of 15°C and a decrease in temperature with height at a rate of 2°C/1,000 feet up to a height of 36,000 ft. Temperature is assumed to be constant above this height. Barometric pressure alters from day to day and area to area so that provision is made for setting the altimeter by means of a small knob at the bottom of the instrument. This is adjusted in conjunction with a **Sub-Scale** on the face of the instrument, the scale being calibrated in millibars or inches of mercury.

Altimeter Settings

On request Air Traffic Control will give the pilot an altimeter setting (in millibars or inches of mercury as required) which can take the following forms—

1. QFE. With this setting the altimeter will read zero when the aircraft is on the ground regardless of the height of the aerodrome above sea level. This setting enables the pilot to know how far he must descend before touch down. On the QFE setting vertical distance above the ground is reported as a **Height**.

2. QNH. Barometric pressure may vary quite considerably from one area to another particularly when a depression with steep pressure gradients covers the country. The U.K. and surrounding seas are divided into thirteen altimeter setting regions (*Fig.* 24) and a setting for any of these areas is always obtainable from the controlling authority. When a QNH is given this will be the lowest forecast value for the region and with this setting the altimeter will read **Altitude** above sea level enabling the pilot to assess his terrain clearance when in proximity to high ground. When flying from one altimeter setting region to another the pilot must obtain the relevant QNH.

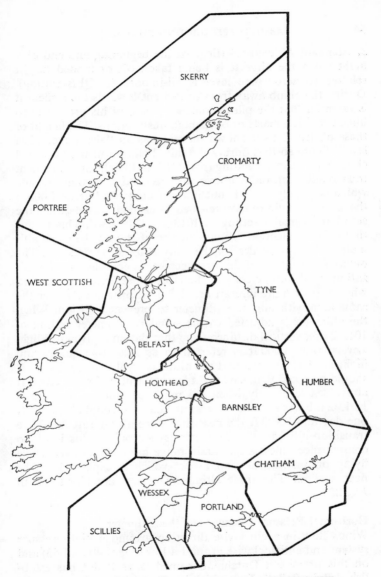

Fig, 24. ALTIMETER SETTING REGIONS OVER THE U.K.

3. Standard Altimeter Setting. At the beginning and end of a flight when the aircraft is being taken off or landed height relative to aerodrome level is all-important (QFE setting). During the climb away from or descent towards the airfield it is essential that the pilot should be aware of his proximity to hills, television masts or other high obstructions. The height of these obstructions is shown on maps as an "above mean sea level" figure so that during the initial climb out the pilot will change his altimeter setting from QFE to QNH, the instrument then reading altitudes above sea level. At a certain altitude which is usually 3,000 ft but in some controlled areas 4,000 ft the aircraft is said to have reached **Transition Altitude** when the standard altimeter setting of 1013·2 will be used. This means that above transition altitude all aircraft fly on the same altimeter setting regardless of the daily barometric pressure. The obvious advantage of this arrangement is complete synchronization of all altimeters and therefore more certain separation when two or more aircraft are flying on instruments over the same area with only the altimeter to prevent collision. When the altimeter is adjusted to the standard altimeter setting of 1013·2 mb, vertical distance from that datum is given in **Flight Levels**: thus 4,000 ft is referred to as FLIGHT LEVEL 40 and flight level 150 means that the altimeter will read 15,000 ft. It should be noted that, say, flight level 80 will in fact be 8,000 ft above sea level only when the m.s.l. barometric pressure is 1,013·2 mb. As a result of pressure changes it could be 8,300 ft one day and 7,900 ft the next, but since all aircraft fly above transition altitude with altimeters synchronized this is of no consequence unless a mountain range has to be crossed while flying on instruments, an aspect which is explained in the next section. The three altimeter settings are illustrated in *Fig.* 25.

Horizontal Pressure Changes and the Altimeter

Winds flow in a clockwise direction around a high-pressure system and anticlockwise around a low (pages 40 and 43) and on this premise a Dutchman named Buys Ballot has established **Buys Ballot's Law** which in effect says:

"In the northern hemisphere if you stand with your back to the wind the area of low pressure is on your left."

The significance of this statement and its effect upon the behaviour of the altimeter may best be understood with reference to *Fig.* 26. This illustrates an aircraft on a cross-country flight which passes over a 2,740 ft ridge of hills. The pilot has decided to fly at an altitude of 3,000 ft, only allowing 260ft terrain clearance over the highest point. Had he studied the

STANDARD
SETTING
'flight level'

TRANSITION   ALTITUDE

QNH
'altitude'

QFE
'height'

Fig. 25. ALTIMETER SETTINGS

weather map before the flight the pilot would have seen that his track led into a region of lower barometric pressure than that at the point of departure. The pilot maintains a constant indicated altitude of 3,000 ft but owing to the decreasing pressure the aircraft assumes a gradual descent.

A change in pressure of one millibar will alter the reading on the altimeter by 30 ft. In this case after flying 50 miles the m.s.l. pressure has dropped from 1,007 mb at the aerodrome of departure (Point *A*) to 1,002 mb, i.e. a pressure decrease of 5 mb or 5 × 30 = 150 ft **Over-read**. After the next 50 miles there is a further pressure reduction to 997 mb or 10 mb below the original altimeter setting of 10 mb or 10 × 30 = 300 ft **Over-read** so that although a steady 3,000 ft reading is maintained on the altimeter the aircraft has in fact descended to

2,700 ft a.m.s.l. and is therefore unable to clear the range of hills which on this occasion happens to be in cloud. As a guiding principle it is worth remembering that according to Buys Ballot's Law an aircraft experiencing starboard drift is flying

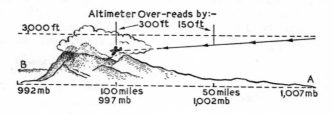

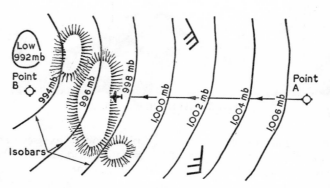

Fig. 26. BEHAVIOUR OF ALTIMETER WHEN FLYING INTO LOWER PRESSURE

towards an area of lower pressure and the altimeter will over-read (*Fig.* 27). Conversely when there is port drift the aircraft is flying into higher pressure and the altimeter will under-read so that starboard drift may reduce terrain clearance to the point of danger while port drift will increase the safety margin between aircraft and high ground (these rules are reversed in

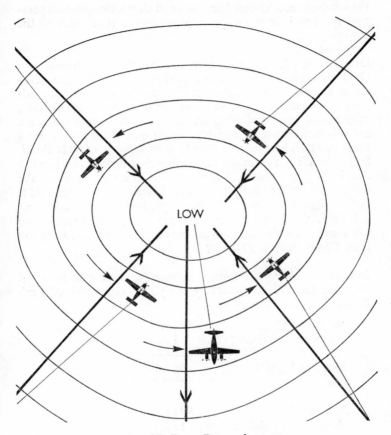

Fig. 27. Buys Ballot's law

All single-engined aircraft are flying towards the area of low pressure and have starboard drift. The twin is flying towards higher pressure (port drift).

the southern hemisphere because wind circulation around pressure systems is in the opposite direction to that north of the equator).

Determining Circuit Height at the Destination Aerodrome

On a cross-country flight the departure and destination aerodromes are usually at different elevations. Furthermore horizontal pressure changes, as explained in the previous section, may have a profound effect on the altimeter so that when the flight is in a non-radio aircraft due allowance for both factors must be made by the pilot if he is to establish a 1,000 ft circuit before landing. For example, assume that the aircraft has left Southend Aerodrome (25 ft above m.s.l.) on a day when the QFE is 994 mb. If the pilot has set his altimeter to read 25 ft before take-off at what indicated height must he fly to complete a 1,000 ft circuit around Luton aerodrome (500 ft a.m.s.l.) and what will the altimeter read on landing there when Luton are reporting a QFE of 974 mb?

METHOD. First reduce both aerodrome pressures to sea-level pressure (i.e. QFE to QNH) by applying a correction of 1 mb for every 30 ft of elevation—

Southend QFE	994 mb
Aerodrome height 25 ft	1 mb
Southend QNH	995 mb

Luton QFE	974 mb
Aerodrome height 500 ft	17 mb
Luton QNH	991 mb

From these simple calculations it will be seen that sea-level pressure at Southend is 4 mb greater than that at Luton, this representing a difference of 4 × 30 or 120 ft in altimeter reading. In this case the flight is towards lower pressure and the altimeter will therefore over-read by 120 ft so that to fly a 1,000 ft circuit around Luton the instrument must read

Height required	1,000 ft
Aerodrome elevation	500
Instrument over-read due to 4 mb pressure difference between Luton and Southend	120
Indicated height	1,620 ft

On landing at Luton the altimeter will read 620 ft, i.e. aerodrome height a.m.s.l. plus the 120 ft over-read resulting from the pressure difference between Southend and Luton.

Radio-equipped aircraft would normally obtain a QFE from Luton Tower frequency so that on landing the altimeter would read zero.

CHAPTER 3

Navigation

The Earth
For the purposes of navigation the earth may be regarded as a sphere covered by a network of lines called meridians and parallels of latitude. **Meridians** (also termed lines of longitude) are semicircles joining the north and south geographical poles through the equator. **Parallels of Latitude** are circles on the earth parallel to the equator.

Any point on the surface of the earth may be defined in relation to these fixed references using as measurement degrees (°), minutes (′) and when very high accuracy is required, seconds (″). **Latitude** is measured north or south of the equator (the equator being 0° and the poles 90°) while **Longitude** is measured east or west of the prime meridian which runs through Greenwich, the prime meridian being 0° and 180° its opposite meridian on the other side of the earth. Such a position is usually called a LAT and LONG, that shown at point *X* (*Fig.* 28) being 59°N 60°W. To quote a specific example the LAT and LONG of Redhill aerodrome is 51° 14′N 00° 08′W.

Variation
In the paragraph dealing with latitude and longitude it was explained that one of the main reference points is the north geographical pole, or **True North** as it is called.

Meridians drawn on aeronautical charts all extend towards true north, and any direction measured on such charts will be a true direction. However, a compass needle influenced solely by the earth's magnetic field does not point towards true north, but instead takes up a direction towards magnetic north—a position in Baffinland in North-eastern Canada many miles from the north geographical pole. Furthermore, this magnetic pole is not fixed but is moving very gradually round the true pole. Thus the direction indicated by a compass needle will alter in relation to true north each year, although the change is very small. In Great Britain the annual change is about 7′

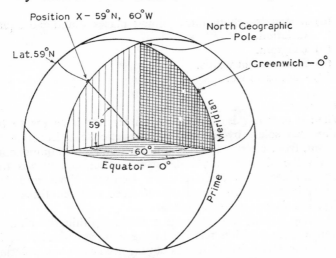

Fig. 28. LATITUDE AND LONGITUDE

east. This difference, between the direction of true north and magnetic north is known as **Variation**.

The amount of angular difference alters from place to place and may be east or west of true north. For example, the variation in Burma and Western Australia is nil, whereas at Vancouver Island it is 25°E and on the other side of Canada, in Newfoundland, it is over 30°W.

To sum up: variation is the angular difference between the true meridian and the magnetic meridian. The size of this angle depends on

(*a*) Position of the compass on the earth's surface.

(*b*) The date, because the magnetic pole is not static. (The date of the variation and the annual change is stated on all charts.)

The method of showing variation on charts may be in the form of

(*a*) Isogonals—chain lines joining places that have equal variation.
(*b*) Diagram.
(*c*) Statement in words.
(*d*) Compass rose.

Deviation

When a compass is installed in an aircraft it ceases to be influenced solely by the earth's magnetic field. Local magnetism, from electrical wiring and iron and steel components within the aircraft, has a disturbing effect and causes the compass needle to point towards **Compass North** and not **Magnetic North**. The angular difference between these two directions is known as **Deviation**.

During a turn the magnetic materials within the aircraft change their position relative to the compass needle, or, in other words, the aircraft moves but the needle remains pointing to compass north. Consequently, deviation will alter with the heading of the aircraft; e.g. on a course of 090° deviation may be 3°W and on a reciprocal course (270°) it may be 3°E, while at some point between these headings it will be nil. Every aircraft compass is fitted with adjustable compensating magnets positioned in a **Corrector Box** attached to the underside of the compass bowl. By manipulating the magnets with a key it is possible to reduce deviation to a minimum, but it cannot be eliminated entirely. For the pilot's information, therefore, a card is tabulated with the amount of deviation remaining after correcting adjustments have been made. This **Deviation Card** is mounted in a frame provided in the cockpit.

With deviation minimized and the final values recorded, the compass can still be influenced by the metal objects in its vicinity. A bag of golf clubs unwittingly stowed near the compass can easily put an aircraft many miles off its Required Track.

Allowing for Variation and Deviation. Consider what must be done to convert a true heading—Hdg.(T)—into a compass

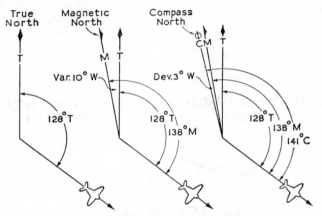

Fig. 29. VARIATION AND DEVIATION

heading—Hdg.(C)—or, in other words, how is allowance made for both variation and deviation?

Having found variation and deviation it only remains for the pilot to determine whether the figures should be added or subtracted to the true course to find Hdg.(C)—the course to steer on the compass. The simple rule of application may be remembered by the words

"East is least and West is best."

In other words deduct easterly variation and deviation and add if westerly.

Fig. 29 illustrates the procedure. Hdg.(T) is shown as the angle between true north and the direction in which the aircraft is heading—in this case 128°. The second sketch shows 10°W

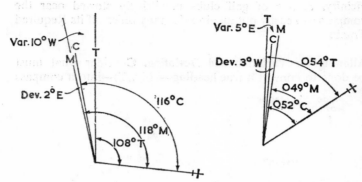

Fig. 30. FINDING Hdg.(M) AND Hdg.(C)

Fig. 31. FINDING Hdg.(M) AND Hdg.(T)

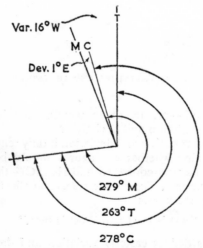

Fig. 32. FINDING Hdg.(C) AND Hdg.(T)

variation added to Hdg.(T) to produce a Hdg.(M) of 138°.
From the correction card in the cockpit deviation on this
course is 3°W, i.e. three degrees west of magnetic north.
Further reference to *Fig.* 29 will show that the W variation
added to obtain the correct Hdg.(C)—141°.

When converting Hdg.(C) to Hdg.(T) calculations have to be
reversed.

Complete the following examples for practice—

	Hdg.(T)	Var.	Hdg.(M)	Dev.	Hdg.(C)	
(1)	108°	10°W	?	2°E	?	(*Fig.* 30)
(2)	324°	13°W	?	1°W	?	
(3)	?	5°E	?	3°W	052°	(*Fig.* 31)
(4)	?	8°W	?	1°E	183°	
(5)	?	16°W	279°	1°E	?	(*Fig.* 32)
(6)	?	5°E	358°	3°W	?	

ANSWERS: (1) Hdg.(M), 118°; Hdg.(C), 116°. (2) Hdg.(M), 337°;
Hdg.(C), 338°. (3) Hdg.(M), 049°; Hdg.(T), 054°. (4) Hdg.(M), 184°;
Hdg.(T), 176°. (5) Hdg.(T), 263°; Hdg.(C), 278°. (6) Hdg.(T), 003°;
Hdg.(C), 001°.

Locating and Plotting Positions

Before flying from one point to another it is first necessary to
find both positions on a chart. This is easy when each position
is an aerodrome or geographical feature shown on the chart.
Sometimes, however, the pilot may be confronted with the
problem of flying to a map reference point given as a latitude
and longitude, or he may have to plot two positions to solve a
navigational problem, as is required in the examination for the
Private Pilot's Licence.

In the introductory paragraph to this chapter the network
system of meridians and parallels of latitude was explained
and this knowledge can now be applied in locating a latitude
and longitude position on a chart. As an example, imagine a
flight from position *A* (53° 59′N, 02° 17′W) to position *B*
(53° 00′N, 03° 46′W)—*Fig.* 33.

METHOD
(*a*) Select a suitable map.
(*b*) To plot position *A* find latitude 53°, then step off the

odd minutes of arc with a pair of dividers on the marginal graduations.

(c) Transfer this distance and make a small pin-prick as near to 02° 17′W as can be estimated.

(d) Set the dividers to seventeen minutes on the nearest graduated parallel to the position. Transfer the dividers to the estimated position and make a larger pin-prick exactly on the position.

(e) Circle the position and mark it thus

⊙ Posn. *A* 53° 59′N
02° 17′W

(f) Plot and mark position *B* in a similar manner.

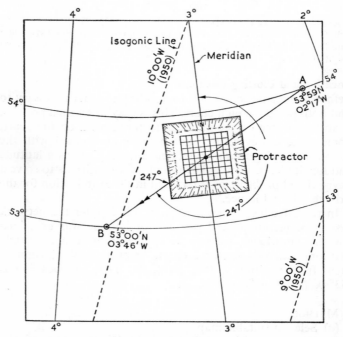

Fig. 33. MEASURING THE REQUIRED TRACK

Measuring Direction

With the points of departure and destination located on the map now join them with a straight line. This is called the **Required Track** (Rqd. Tr.), and its direction is measured in degrees relative to true north but certain precautions must be taken. From *Fig.* 33 it can be seen that one of the properties of the maps used for pilot navigation is the convergence of the meridians towards the nearer pole, so any line drawn across the chart will intersect each successive meridian at a slightly different angle. The **Convergence** on the actual charts will not be as great as that shown in the illustration. Even so, over relatively long distances, particularly on tracks running east/west, convergence should be allowed for by measuring the direction of the Rqd. Tr. on the meridian nearest to half-way along the line in order to obtain a mean direction. For the actual measuring a protractor is needed—the 360° Douglas protractor/parallel rule being ideal for this purpose.

METHOD (*Fig.* 33 *refers*)

(*a*) Join point of departure to destination with a straight line and label it with the double arrow.

(*b*) Place the small hole at the centre of the protractor on the Reqd. Tr. and align the 0°/180° graduations over the meridian nearest to half-way along track.

(*c*) Reading clockwise from 0° find the direction of the Reqd. Tr.

(*d*) Make a note of the direction in the **Flight Log**. It is advisable to leave out the degree symbol (°) when making an entry, as this hurriedly written in the air may be mistaken for a nought.

(*e*) At the same time make a note of the magnetic variation over the route. On short flights the reading from an isogonal half-way along the route will do, but on longer journeys it is more accurate to adjust course as variation alters. In either case, remember to allow for the annual change when taking the reading from an isogonal on the map.

Measuring Distances

Having measured and noted the direction of the Rqd. Tr. (247° in *Fig.* 33), next measure the distance between the two points. The units selected should correspond with the calibration of the air-speed indicator—that is, if it is calibrated in knots, measure in nautical miles; if calibrated in m.p.h., measure in statute miles.

METHOD

(*a*) Set the legs of the dividers to a convenient span on the graduated scale line at the foot of the chart or at the graduated margins.

(*b*) Step off the distance along the Track adding on any odd span at the end to complete the procedure.

(*c*) Make a note of the distance in the flight log. Assume that in *Fig.* 33 the distance is 145 statute miles.

WIND			NOTES						
HEIGHT	FROM°T	SPEED							
FROM		TO	T.A.S.	Ht.	RqdTr.	Hdg(M)	Dist.	G/S	Time
A		B	122	4,000	247	257	145	122	1·11

Fig. 34. A TYPICAL FLIGHT LOG

Zero Wind Dead Reckoning

Dead Reckoning (D.R.) is the planned navigational strategy for a cross-country flight. The details—Rqd. Tr., distance, variation, height to fly, etc.—are taken into account and the results of the reckoning are recorded in the flight log, a typical example being illustrated in *Fig.* 34. Often during a cross-country flight, modifications and alterations will have to be made to the plan. Actual wind speed or direction, or maybe both, is frequently different from that used when computing calculations on the ground. Perhaps a diversion may be necessary to avoid a thunderstorm, or a technical defect may make it prudent to land earlier than expected.

Before introducing the effects of wind speed and direction, for purpose of instruction imagine a cross-country flight between positions *A* and *B* (*Fig.* 33) in conditions of no wind. Having plotted the two positions, drawn in the Rqd. Tr., measured it for bearing and distance and determined the variation the following must be found to complete the pre-flight log—

> True air-speed (T.A.S.)
> Ground speed (G/S)
> Time (i.e. duration of flight)
> Magnetic Heading (Hdg.(M))

METHOD

(*a*) It is first necessary to determine the True Air-speed (T.A.S.). Assuming it is intended to cruise the aircraft at an Indicated Air-speed (I.A.S.) of 115 m.p.h. and the instrument correction card shows an error of -1, the Rectified Air-speed (R.A.S.) will be 114 m.p.h. Both height and outside air temperature will affect the R.A.S. but the correction is made simple with the aid of a navigational computer and the procedure is explained on page 102. In this example assume T.A.S. is 122 m.p.h.

(*b*) In a dead calm the speed of the aircraft over the ground (ground speed) will be the same as the speed through the air (true air-speed); in this example, 122 m.p.h.

(*c*) The time to cover the distance from *A* to *B*—145 statute miles—depends on the ground speed of the aircraft.

$$\therefore \quad \text{time} = \frac{145}{122} \times \frac{60}{1} \text{ min} = 1 \text{ hr } 11 \text{ min}$$

Height corrections and time over distance calculations may likewise be quickly solved on a navigational computer and this is explained later in the chapter.

(d) In this case 10° westerly variation must be added to 247°, making a magnetic track of 257°.

(e) Without wind to make the aircraft drift either to port or starboard the Hdg.(T) will be the same as the Rqd. Tr. In other words, the nose of the aircraft should point directly towards the destination throughout the flight. Applying variation as in (d) the Hdg.(M) is found −257°.

Wind Effect

The effect of wind on an aircraft in flight must now be considered. It is most important that the fundamentals of this

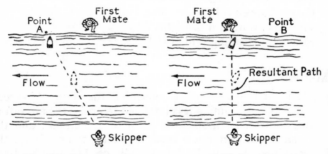

Fig. 35. THE EFFECT OF DRIFT AND (right) CORRECTIVE ACTION

problem are realized and grasped, for they are applied on practically all cross-country flights. Windless days are very rare indeed, and wind itself is a fickle thing, changing in both speed and direction from place to place and from time to time, often hourly.

In ordinary flight the wind does not have any effect on an aircraft's attitude, flying characteristics or air-speed. What it does influence, however, and often to a marked extent, is the relative motion of the aircraft to the ground. For example, a wind from either the port or starboard side of the aircraft will make it travel over the ground, not in the direction in which it is heading but with a tendency to **drift** to one side. When near the ground this crabbing motion may at first be disconcerting, but remember to look well ahead in the direction in which the aircraft is going and not over the nose where the aircraft is heading, or pointing.

This study of drift may be compared with the model motor-boat plying between two boys directly opposite each other on the banks of a river. In his first attempt to navigate his craft across the river, the "Skipper" aims his boat straight towards his "First Mate" and blithely ignores the current, with the result that the boat reaches the opposite bank at *A*, five yards downstream of the intended destination (*Fig.* 35). After some deliberation and consultation it is decided that the boat should be headed partly into the current of the river, so on his second attempt the "Skipper" aims his boat at point *B*, approximately five yards upstream of the "First Mate." The resultant path now makes a near right-angle with the bank. A boat floats on water and an aircraft is supported in air but the effect of drift is the same in each case.

As may be expected, the wind will not always lie on the aircraft's beam. It may be blowing obliquely to the fore-and-aft axis or it may so happen, for example, that a cross-country flight is made against a head wind. As always, the air-speed will then remain the same, but the aircraft's speed relative to the ground (ground speed) will be equivalent to the air-speed *minus* the wind speed. When flying with a tail or following wind the ground speed will be the air-speed *plus* the wind speed. In both these latter instances there will be no drift if the aircraft is headed dead into or out of the eye of the wind.

The Three Vectors in the Triangle of Velocities
The movement or velocity of an aircraft travelling in a straight line at a uniform speed can be represented by a line drawn to a chosen scale. This is called a **Vector**. It represents not only the speed of the aircraft but also the direction in which it is moving when drawn in relation to a fixed datum—true north.

For ordinary cross-country flights navigational problems

will entail three velocities, each involving a pair of variable factors. They are

1. Heading true and true air-speed
2. Wind speed and direction
3. Track and ground speed

When drawn in relation to one another all three vectors representing these velocities make the **Triangle of Velocities**. In the following pages will be solved examples of navigational problems by the plotting method in which the vectors are drawn, and later, by using a navigational computer. Provided four of the six factors are known the remaining two "unknowns" may be found by the triangle of velocities. Once he understands this basic method of solving navigational problems the student will find little difficulty in mastering one of the navigational computers, a valuable tool of the pilot-navigator. For example, when the course true, true air-speed, wind speed and direction are known by plotting these component velocities and then determining the resultant velocity, track and ground speed will be found.

To make speedier entries in the air, abbreviations are used, most of which are given on pages ix to xi. The shortened method of entering the six factors is

Heading true　.　　.　　.　　.　　.	Hdg.(T)
True air-speed .　　.　　.　　.　　.	T.A.S.
Wind speed and direction .　　.　　.	W/V
(Wind velocity)	
Required track.　　.　　.　　.　　.	Rqd. Tr. or Tr. Req.
Track made good　.　　.　　.　　.	T.M.G.
Ground speed .　　.　　.　　.　　.	G/S

Lastly, before proceeding with some practical problems, a word on the importance of accuracy. For boys and their motor-boats an error of two or three degrees is of no account, but in air navigation an error of only one degree will account for an aircraft being one mile off its Rqd. Tr. after it has travelled sixty miles (see page 104).

In all workings, whether with protractor, dividers or when using a computer or slide-rule, endeavour to work to the nearest whole degree of arc, the nearest half-minute of time and the nearest half-mile of distance. An arrival exactly over the destination dead on E.T.A. is ample reward for the extra care.

1. How to Find Hdg.(T) and G/S (and Drift). For this example assume that a flight is planned from Exeter to Christchurch. Weather conditions are a little uncertain, so a check is made with the nearest meteorological station. The Duty Forecaster is able to provide an accurate route forecast and advises that the wind velocity at 2,000 ft is from 225° with a speed of 30 m.p.h. Remember that the wind direction is always given as that from which the wind blows. The temperature at 2,000 ft is 25°C, so there is no danger of icing. This temperature figure will be used to compute the T.A.S.

Next locate both aerodromes on the chart, and join them with a straight line to establish the Rqd. Tr.; this is marked with the double-arrow symbol pointing in the direction of the destination. Following this measure the direction by aligning the 0°/180° line on the protractor with a meridian approximately half-way between Exeter and Christchurch and with the centre hole over the Rqd. Tr. line. Counting clockwise from N read off 090°. This figure is noted in the pre-flight log. There are now four known factors: viz. W/V, 225°/30 m.p.h.; Rqd. Tr., 090°; and the T.A.S., which, when computed, is 90 m.p.h. These four "knowns" are used to construct a triangle of velocities and so find the remaining two unknown factors, i.e. Hdg.(T) and G/S (*Fig. 36*).

METHOD

(*a*) With the protractor centred on Exeter aerodrome and parallel to an adjacent meridian, mark the direction of the wind vector *downwind* from the aerodrome, i.e. away from 225°.

(*b*) Choose a suitable scale—one which is big enough to be accurate and yet small enough to allow the resultant vector to be spanned with the dividers—then with the origin at Exeter scale off 30 m.p.h. with the dividers along the wind vector. Label the vector with triple arrows pointing with the wind.

(c) With radius equivalent to 90 m.p.h. (T.A.S.) and with the extremity of the wind vector as centre, strike an arc or make a small pin-prick so as to cut the Rqd. Tr.

(d) Form the Hdg.(T)/T.A.S. vector by joining with a straight line the extremity of the wind vector and the intersection on the Rqd. Tr. Label with a single arrow as in *Fig.* 36.

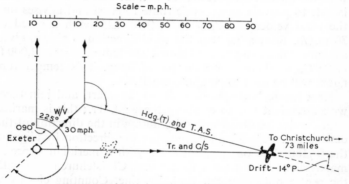

Fig. 36. FINDING Hdg.(T), G/S AND DRIFT

(*Note.* The wind and course arrows when pursued around the triangle should always oppose in direction the double-arrow symbol of Track.)

(e) With the protractor centred and aligned measure the direction of the Hdg.(T)—104°. Span the Tr. and G/S vector (between Exeter and intersection) and apply this to the scale to find the G/S—109 m.p.h.

(f) With the dividers set to a convenient distance on the graduated border of the chart, step off the distance from Exeter to Christchurch—73 miles—and record figure in pre-flight log. Compute or calculate time to travel 73 miles at a G/S of 109 m.p.h.

2. How to Find Tr. and G/S (and Drift). After setting course from Shoreham airport at a T.A.S. of 100 knots on a Hdg.(T) of 114°, a wind velocity of 017°/25 kt is transmitted to the aircraft by Shoreham Tower.

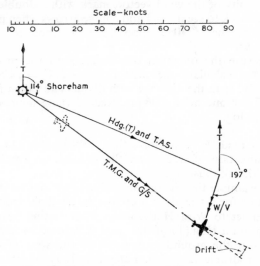

Fig. 37. Finding Track, G/S and Drift

With the aid of these two vectors (Hdg.(T)/T.A.S. and W/V) now construct a triangle of velocities and find the two unknowns—Tr. and G/S (*Fig.* 37).

Method

(*a*) With the protractor orientated, aligned and centred on Shoreham airport, mark the direction of the Hdg.(T) and T.A.S. vector and draw a line of any length.

(*b*) Using a convenient scale mark off along the line a distance equivalent to one hour's air-speed. Label the vector with an arrow.

(*c*) With the protractor centred on the extremity of the Hdg.(T) and T.A.S. vector, mark the direction of the wind vector; this should be *with the wind*. Now scale off along this line the equivalent of one hour's wind speed. Label with triple arrows pointing with the wind.

(d) Draw in the Tr. by joining Shoreham airport to the extremity of the wind vector, mark with a double arrow and check to see if wind and course arrows when pursued around the triangle oppose the direction of the Tr. arrows.

(e) Measure the direction of the Tr. with the protractor (128°), calculate the drift (128° − 114° = 14°S) and, finally, span the distance with dividers and then find the G/S for one hour (106 kt). Record these figures in the flight log.

3. How to Find W/V. To solve this problem Hdg.(T), T.A.S. and the direction of track over the ground, or **Track Made Good** (T.M.G.), must be known.

In this example the student should assume that he is acting as navigator for a friend on a cross-country flight from Sherburn-in-Elmet to West Hartlepool. After setting heading at 10.37 a.m. on a Hdg.(T) of 014° at a T.A.S. of 94 m.p.h. the T.M.G. over the ground passes just to the west of Church Fenton aerodrome (*Fig*. 38). Later a railway is crossed and off on the starboard beam York is easily recognizable. At 10.45 a.m. another railway, which runs nearly at right-angles to the T.M.G., is crossed. Almost immediately afterwards a rectangular wood on the south side of a river is pin-pointed; then another railway passes below. At 10.51 a.m. a good pin-point occurs exactly over a village where a single-track railway terminates. The flight log up to this moment should read something like that shown in *Fig*. 39.

Now that position has been established with certainty an attempt may be made to find the W/V.

METHOD

(a) Draw in the T.M.G. from Sherburn-in-Elmet to the village.

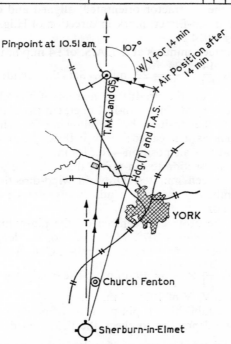

Fig. 38. FINDING THE WIND VELOCITY DURING FLIGHT

TIME	OBSERVATION	E.T.A.
10·37	S/H WEST HARTLEPOOL. 014 (T)	11·15
10·45	x rlwy YORK to stb.	
10·51	p.p. village G/S 101 mph	11·12
	W/V 107/19	

Fig. 39. IN-FLIGHT OBSERVATIONS RELATING TO *Fig.* 38.

87

(b) With the protractor orientated, aligned and centred on Sherburn-in-Elmet, mark in direction of Hdg.(T)/T.A.S. vector—014°.

(c) In fourteen minutes at a T.A.S. of 94 m.p.h. the aircraft covers $\frac{14}{60} \times \frac{94}{1} = 22$ miles. Set the dividers to this distance on the graduated margin of the chart, then, with centre on Sherburn-in-Elmet, cut the course vector. This is the position before allowing for wind, or **Air Position** as it is called; mark it thus, △, and enter the time at this air position—10.51 a.m.

(d) Join intersection to pin-point; this gives the wind vector for fourteen minutes. Draw in wind-direction arrows, remembering that the wind always blows from course to track.

(e) With the protractor centred on the pin-point, measure wind direction—107°. Measure, too, the length of the wind vector—four and a half miles. Converted to m.p.h. this is $\frac{4\frac{1}{2}}{14} \times \frac{60}{1} = 19$ m.p.h. The navigator will have found a W/V of 107°/19 m.p.h.

(f) After establishing a pin-point and finding a new W/V, it is good practice to check the E.T.A. at destination—

Distance to run = 36 miles
G/S = 101 m.p.h.

∴   Time = $\frac{36}{101} \times \frac{60}{1} = 21$ min

E.T.A. West Hartlepool = 11.12 a.m.

THE NAVIGATIONAL COMPUTER

In the preceding pages the triangle of velocity was used to solve navigational problems by plotting to scale the three all-important vectors, viz. track and ground speed, heading (T) and true air-speed and wind speed and direction.

The computer eliminates all this plotting, and when it is used in conjunction with the circular slide-rule (usually incorporated in the computer) most navigational problems can be solved easily, quickly and with a high degree of accuracy.

Construction of Computer

The Dalton Navigational Computer which became so well known to the wartime service pilot incorporated a moving belt overprinted with drift lines. The instrument was contained within a rather cumbersome metal box and it has now been superseded by the modern lightweight computer which although based upon the Dalton is nevertheless small enough to be carried in a flat briefcase. Most of these computers can perform two main functions—

1. The solving of triangle of velocity problems.
2. Time and distance calculations together with various conversions. These will be explained later in the chapter.

A typical modern computer is illustrated in *Fig*. 40. It is constructed of white plastic, each side being designed to perform the two functions previously mentioned. Dealing with triangle of velocity problems first the relevant part of the computer consists of a rotatable compass rose which may be set against a pointer or **True Heading Arrow** at the top of the computer. Attached to the compass rose is a circular transparent plotting area. It has a matt surface so that it can be marked with soft pencil or ink. Ball point pens are to be avoided since they can prove difficult to erase from the surface. Since the plotting area is attached to the compass rose it follows that both components rotate together.

Located in slots within the body of the computer is a movable oblong sheet of plastic overprinted with drift lines or **Fan Lines** which originate from a common point. These are crossed by a series of **Speed Arcs** (also drawn from a common centre) marked in figures from 20 to 250 while the reverse side of the slide is calibrated from 150 to 750 for high speed aircraft. These figures may be regarded as kilometres per hour, miles per hour or knots as required. As this calibrated slide is moved up or down in the computer the markings and figures appear behind the rotatable transparent plotting area.

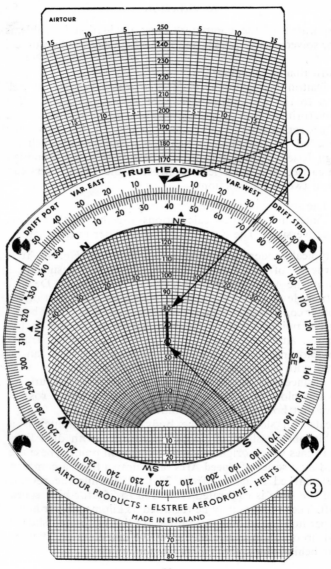

The only permanent mark on the plotting area is a small central dot. In a serviceable computer this should remain over the centre line of the calibrated slide when the compass rose is rotated. Should it wander off centre accuracy will suffer accordingly.

1. How to Find Hdg.(T) and G/S (and Drift). Assume that a flight is from Yeadon, near Leeds, to Squires Gate, Blackpool. The Rqd. Tr. is 263°, and the most economical cruising speed is 120 m.p.h. Cruising altitude is fixed at 3,000 ft. The wind velocity at this height is known to be 038°/20 m.p.h. What will be the Co.(T), G/S and drift?

METHOD

(a) Set the W/V by rotating the compass rose until direction 038° is aligned against the "true heading" arrow. Using the centre line of the sliding scale as a measuring rule make a small ink or pencil mark on the plotting area 20 units UP from the central dot (a line is shown in the illustration but a dot is more convenient). The wind velocity has now been set on the computer (*Fig.* 40).

(b) Set the Rqd. Tr. on the computer by rotating the compass rose until 263° is against the true heading arrow. Wind Velocity and Required Track are now set in relation to one another.

(c) Set the T.A.S. by moving the sliding scale until the 120 arc is directly under the ink or pencil dot (*Fig.* 41).

(d) To find the Hdg.(T) it only remains to determine its angular difference port or starboard of Track. Reference to the sliding scale shows the ink dot to be on the 7° starboard fan line indicating that Heading is 7°S of Track.

Fig. 40. FINDING HEADING AND GROUND SPEED: STAGE 1

(1) Set wind direction.
(2) Mark wind speed using sliding scale to measure up from central dot (3).

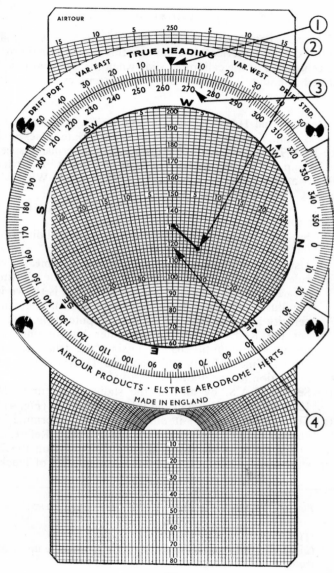

Surrounding the top portion of the compass rose is a scale marked in degrees port and starboard of the true heading arrow. Transfer the reading from the fan lines to this scale and under the 7° starboard mark read off the True Heading, in this case 270°.

(e) The central dot on the plotting area indicates the ground speed which is 133 m.p.h.

Note. Finding a Hdg.(T) and G/S from a W/V, T.A.S., and Rqd. Tr. is the most common requirement of the pilot/navigator. The foregoing procedure represents a major departure from the method usually taught. It eliminates the trial and error procedure used in the older method for finding drift and is in consequence both simpler and quicker.

2. How to Find W/V when Tr. and G/S are Known. After making good a track parallel to the railway which leaves Boston, Lincs, on a bearing of 038° (T), G/S is found to be 100 m.p.h. The Hdg.(T) is 048° and T.A.S. is 90 m.p.h. Compute the W/V for the height at which the aircraft is flying.

METHOD

(a) Set Hdg.(T) against true heading arrow.

(b) Set T.A.S. below dot on plotting dial.

(c) Calculate the drift with the aid of the computer or mentally, viz. Tr. = 038°, Hdg.(T) = 048°, therefore Drift = 10° P.

Fig. 41. FINDING HEADING AND GROUND SPEED: STAGE 2

(1) Set Required Track. Using the speed arcs (4) set T.A.S. under wind velocity mark and determine drift from nearest fan line (2).

(3) Transfer drift to drift scale (above the compass ring) and True Heading will be found immediately below in this case 270°.

Ground Speed shown under central dot is 133 m.p.h.

(*d*) Make W/V mark where 10° P. drift line intersects the 100 m.p.h. ground speed arc. (*Fig.* 42.)

(*e*) Rotate plotting dial until W/V mark is on the centre line in the lower half of the computer.

(*f*) Read wind direction against true heading arrow—165°.

(*g*) Read wind speed by counting the units, and fraction of units if any, between dot and W/V mark—20 m.p.h. (*Fig.* 43.)

3. How to Find T.M.G. and G/S. For this example assume that the pilot has set heading from Lympne on 136° (T). T.A.S. is 139 kt and the W/V is 240/30 kt. In order to determine where he shall cross the French coast he must compute the T.M.G. (track-made-good, over the ground or sea). To find the E.T.A. it will also be necessary to know the G/S.

METHOD

(*a*) Set W/V by rotating the compass rose until 240 is adjacent to the true heading arrow, then make an ink dot 30 units **down** from the central dot.

(*b*) Set T.A.S. (139 kt) below central dot on plotting dial.

(*c*) Set Hdg.(T) (136°) against true heading arrow.

(*d*) Below W/V mark read amount of drift—11° P. Applied to Hdg.(T), this gives a T.M.G. of 125°. When plotted on the chart this shows that he should cross the French coast at Ambleteuse, just south of Cape Gris Nez.

(*e*) By reference to the speed arcs a G/S of 149 kt is obtained. As the distance to Ambleteuse is twenty-eight nautical miles, the aircraft will pass over this place after eleven and a quarter minutes' flying.

The Circular Slide-rule (*Fig.* 44)

Attached to the computer, and often used in conjunction with it, is the circular slide-rule. With a little practice this, too, will give speedy and accurate solutions to many of the problems associated with air navigation. The following paragraphs explain how to deal with these problems.

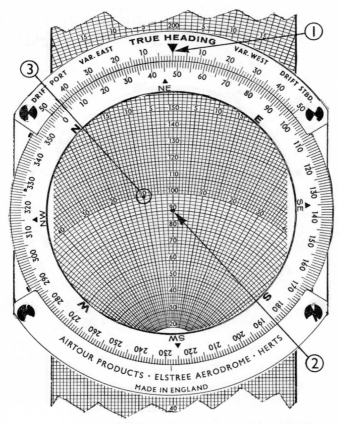

Fig. 42. FINDING W/V FROM A KNOWN Tr. AND G/S:
STAGE 1

(1) Set Hdg.(T) on computer.
(2) Set T.A.S. against central dot.
(3) Place a dot where the known ground speed (speed arc) crosses the known drift (fan line).

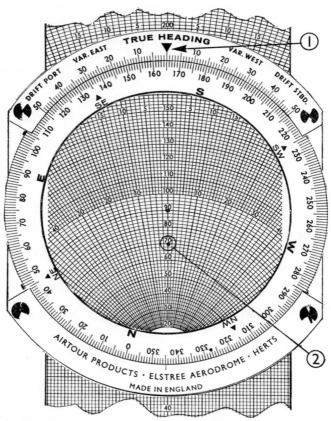

Fig. 43. FINDING W/V FROM A KNOWN Tr. AND G/S:
STAGE 2

Rotate plotting dial until the dot positioned in stage 1
is on the centre line below the centre dot.

(1) Read off wind direction, 165°.
(2) Using the squares on the sliding scale read wind
speed which is 20 m.p.h.

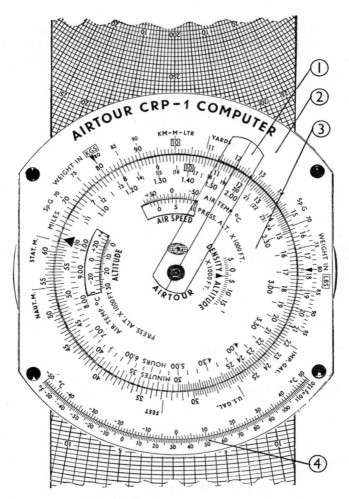

Fig. 44. THE CIRCULAR SLIDE-RULE

Showing the Altimeter and Air-speed Correction
windows and (1) cursor used to help line up outer
scale (2) and rotating inner scale (3). A temperature
conversion scale is also included (4).

1. Calculating Time. On every cross-country flight at least one problem of this nature will occur, e.g. how long (Time) will it take to cover a distance of 225 miles at a G/S of 90 m.p.h.?

Equationally, this is

$$\frac{\text{Distance}}{\text{G/S}} = \text{Time}$$

$$\therefore \qquad \frac{225}{90} = 2\tfrac{1}{2} \text{ hours}$$

Here is a further example of the same type of problem, one which would take several minutes to solve without the aid of a computer.

From Fair Oaks, in Surrey, to Roborough, near Plymouth, the distance is 167 miles. How long would this flight take at a G/S of 93 m.p.h.?

METHOD
(a) Set 60 (minutes) on the inner scale against 93 (miles) on outer scale.
(b) Against 167 on outer scale read on inner scale the number of minutes—108.

2. Calculating Distance. The simple equation now appears in this form

$$\text{G/S} \times \text{Time} = \text{Distance}$$

Here is an example.

After flying for eighteen minutes at a G/S of 87 m.p.h. how far has the aircraft travelled along the fifty-five-mile Track between Birmingham Airport and Cranfield, Beds?

$$\therefore \qquad \frac{87}{1} \times \frac{18}{60} = ? \text{ miles}$$

METHOD

(a) Set 60 on the inner scale against 87 (miles) on the outer scale.

(b) Against 18 (minutes) on inner scale read on outer scale the number of miles—26.

3. Calculating Speed. To find an actual G/S multiply the distance travelled by the time taken, in minutes, to cover the distance.

$$\frac{\text{Distance} \times 60}{\text{Time}} = \text{G/S}$$

Here is an example.

Exactly ten and a half minutes after setting course from Hamble, near Southampton, for Dorchester, the pilot pinpoints himself over Hurn aerodrome. The distance travelled is twenty-three and a half miles. What is the G/S?

$$\frac{23\frac{1}{2} \times 60}{10\frac{1}{2}} = ? \text{ m.p.h.}$$

METHOD

(a) Against $23\frac{1}{2}$ on outer scale set $10\frac{1}{2}$ (minutes) on inner scale.

(b) Against 60 on inner scale read on outer scale the G/S—134 m.p.h.

4. Calculating Fuel Consumption. At economical cruising r.p.m. a particular aircraft uses 4·3 gallons of fuel per hour. How much petrol would be needed for a flight from Denham to Fairwood Common, near Swansea, a distance of $152\frac{1}{2}$ miles, at a G/S of 107 m.p.h.?

METHOD

(a) By calculating as in 1(a) and 1(b) the flight will take 86 min. To this it is good practice to add 20 per cent as a safety precaution against getting lost or having to use an alternative aerodrome.

(b) To find 20 per cent of 86: set 10 (representing 100 per cent) on inner scale against 86 on outer scale. Against 20 on inner scale read off on outer scale 20 per cent of 86 min—17 min. Now proceed to find the amount of fuel required for a flight of 103 min.

(c) Set 60 on inner scale against 4·3 (actually 43) on outer scale.

(d) Against 103 on inner scale read off on outer scale fuel needed—7·4 gallons.

5. Calculating Time and Distance on Fuel Remaining. Here is another type of problem which may be solved on the computer during a cross-country flight.

The fuel gauge indicates that three gallons remain in the tank. How many more minutes' flying will this provide, and how far will the aircraft fly in this time? The fuel consumption and G/S are the same as in the previous example, 4·3 g.p.h. and 107 m.p.h. respectively.

METHOD

(a) Set 60 on inner scale against 4·3 (43) on outer scale.

(b) Against 3 (30) on outer scale read off on inner scale the number of minutes' endurance—42. Now calculate how far the aircraft will fly in these 42 minutes. Here is the procedure.

(c) Set 60 on inner scale against 107 on outer scale.

(d) Against 42 on inner scale read off on outer scale the number of miles—75.

6. Converting Statute Miles, Nautical Miles and Kilometres. There are occasions when it will be necessary to convert statute miles to nautical miles or kilometres, or vice versa. To do this mathematically the following ratios should be memorized—

33 Nautical Miles = 38 Statute Miles = 61 Kilometres

Examples
Convert 88 nautical miles to statute miles.

$$\frac{\overset{8}{\cancel{88}}}{1} \times \frac{38}{\underset{3}{\cancel{33}}} = \frac{304}{3} = 101\tfrac{1}{2} \text{ statute miles}$$

Convert 114 m.p.h. to knots.

$$\frac{\overset{3}{\cancel{114}}}{1} \times \frac{33}{\underset{1}{\cancel{38}}} = 99 \text{ kt}$$

Convert 133 statute miles to kilometres.

$$\frac{\overset{7}{\cancel{133}}}{1} \times \frac{61}{\underset{2}{\cancel{38}}} = \frac{427}{2} = 213\tfrac{1}{2} \text{ km}$$

With the circular slide-rule these problems may be solved within a matter of seconds. While computers differ slightly in detail design the Airtour CRP-I used to illustrate this book has three marks on the outer scale labelled respectively NAUT.M., STAT.M. and KM-M-LTR (representing kilo-metres, metres and litres). When converting units of distance markings on the inner or time scale represent nautical miles, statute miles or kilometres as the case may be. By aligning the NAUT.M. mark against any number of nautical miles (inner scale) the equivalent number of statute miles or kilometres can be read off opposite the appropriate mark. The reverse is equally simple. Similar facilities are provided for converting imperial gallons to U.S. gallons or litres.

Here is an example.

How many statute miles are equivalent to 228 km?

Rotate the inner scale until 228 is in line with the KM mark. Against the STAT.M. mark (*Fig.* 45) read off the equivalent number of statute miles—142.

Air-speed Indicator and Altimeter Corrections

In the chapter on Meteorology it was explained that temperature affected the atmosphere's density which in turn created inaccuracies in the Air-speed Indicator and Altimeter. Additionally the A.S.I. must be compensated for changes in air density which occur with changes in flight level.

Whereas A.S.I. corrections are important even to relatively low-flying aircraft, Altimeter corrections are of more consequence to pilots flying transport aircraft at high cruising levels.

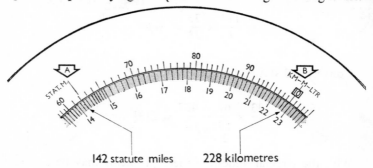

142 statute miles   228 kilometres

Fig. 45. CONVERTING KILOMETRES TO STATUTE MILES
USING THE KILOMETRE MARK (B) AND THE STATUTE MILE
MARK (A) IN CONJUNCTION WITH THE INNER SCALE

Corrections to A.S.I. or Altimeter readings are simple to perform on the circular slide-rule which has two windows provided for the purpose.

METHOD

A.S.I. Corrections (Fig. 46)

Assuming an indicated air-speed (I.A.S.) of 118 kt and an instrument correction of +2 (found on the calibration card in the aircraft) this would give a rectified air-speed (R.A.S.) of 120 kt. If, in this example the aircraft is cruising at 10,000 ft and the outside air temperature (O.A.T.) reads 0°C, set 0° on the scale at the top of the "air-speed" window against figure 10 in the window. The slide-rule is now set to convert any

Fig. 46. FINDING THE TRUE AIR-SPEED

(1) Using the air-speed window set outside air temperature against cruising height.

(2) Find Rectified Air-speed on inner scale and read off True Air-speed on the outer scale, in this example slightly more than 140 kt

R.A.S. to a T.A.S. for that height and temperature. To convert 120 kt R.A.S. locate figure 12 on the rotatable inner scale and the number adjacent to it on the outer scale is the T.A.S., in this case 14 or 140 kt—an appreciable difference of 20 kt.

Altimeter Corrections

Indicated altitude may be corrected to true altitude by setting the reading from the altimeter (using the scale along the bottom of the "altitude" window) against the outside air temperature at that level (figures in the "altitude" window). Conversion from indicated to true is then made reading from inner to outer scale on the circular slide-rule as with air-speed corrections.

For example, the altimeter reads 20,000 ft and the thermometer gives an O.A.T. of $-30°C$. Using the "altitude" window, align 20,000 ft with $-30°$. The circular slide-rule is now set to make the conversion which is completed by locating the indicated altitude on the inner scale and reading true altitude on the outer scale—in this case 19,600 ft.

Units of Measurement

The universal dimension system agreed by the International Civil Aviation Organization (I.C.A.O.) is as follows—

Long distances . .	. Nautical miles and tenths
Short distances (runways, cloud height, poor visibility, ground elevation, etc.)	. Metres
Altitudes and heights .	. Feet
Horizontal speed . .	. Knots
Vertical speed . .	. Feet per minute
Visibility . . .	. Kilometres or metres
Wind-speed and direction	. Degrees and knots
Weight . . .	. Kilogrammes
Temperature . .	. Centigrade

The 1-in-60 Rule

Fig. 47 shows that an error of 1° will account for an aircraft being 1 mile off Track after travelling 60 miles. If this error is not corrected the aircraft will be 2 miles away from its Rqd. Tr. when it has gone twice as far, i.e. 120 miles. Similarly, had the error been 2°, the aircraft would have been 2 miles away from the Rqd. Tr. after 60 miles.

In the example given in *Fig.* 48 it will be seen that a pilot, after flying for 30 miles on a 120-mile leg from *A* to *B*, pinpoints himself at *C*, 3 miles to starboard of his Rqd. Tr.

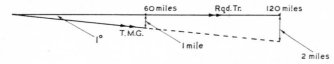

Fig. 47. THE 1-IN-60 RULE

Using the 1-in-60 rule, he calculates his Track error to be 6°. The problem now arises as to how he will regain his Rqd. Tr. As his error is 6°, an alteration by this amount would mean that his new Track will be merely *parallel* to that desired. The 3-mile Track error will remain, and he will arrive at B^1. He

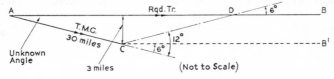

Fig. 48. APPLICATION OF THE RULE—AFTER 30 MILES

must therefore alter heading to port by *double* his Track error, that is, 12°.

After flying for approximately another 30 miles he arrives back on the Reqd. Tr. at *D*, when a further alteration in heading of 6° to starboard is needed to avoid overshooting the Track and to maintain an accurate course to take him to his destination, *B*.

The example in *Fig.* 49 shows that after covering a distance of 15 miles on a 30-mile flight from *X* to *Y*, a pin-point is made at *Z*, 2 miles to port of the Rqd. Tr. What alteration of heading is necessary to reach the destination? Using the 1-in-60 rule, by proportion after 60 miles the aircraft would be 8 miles away from the Rqd. Tr.; therefore, the Track error is 8°. By altering heading to starboard by double this amount the aircraft will converge on to its destination after flying for

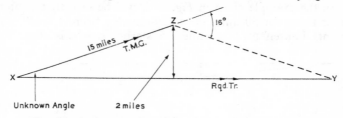

Fig. 49. APPLICATION OF THE RULE—AFTER 15 MILES

approximately the same length of time as it took to reach position Z.

Fig. 50 provides a further situation where another simple rule of thumb will help the pilot-navigator. Assume that the aircraft has covered well over half of the distance to its destination before a Track error of 7° is discovered—in fact,

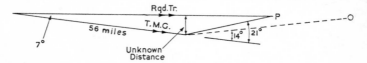

Fig. 50. APPLICATION OF THE RULE—AFTER TWO-THIRDS OF THE DISTANCE

56 miles of an 80-mile flight, or about two-thirds of the total mileage. By simply doubling the Track error and applying this to the heading as in the earlier example, the pilot will arrive at *O*, a considerable distance beyond *P*, his destination. Instead the pilot should apply the rule: *where two-thirds of the distance has been covered, correct by three times the Track error*. In this example, therefore, he would alter heading by 21° to port. While this is not a strictly accurate rule, it is nevertheless good enough for pilot navigation. Yet another method is explained on page 170 of FLIGHT BRIEFING FOR PILOTS, Vol. I.

Making Good a Reciprocal Track (Fig. 51)

Very often a return flight to base will be along the same Track as that used on the outward journey. The Track direction on return, will be the exact opposite, or, in other words, it will be a **Reciprocal** Track, i.e. different by 180° from that measured on the outward journey.

To make good a reciprocal Track a simple rule should be used. It is this: *to the reciprocal Hdg.(T), or Hdg.(M), apply double the drift.* For example, on a flight from Oxford (Kidlington) to Bournemouth (Hurn) the Rqd. Tr. is 198°, Hdg.(T) 188° and the drift 10° starboard. What then is the Hdg.(T) to make good the reciprocal Track of 018° back to Oxford?

METHOD. The reciprocal Hdg.(T) = 188° − 180° = 008°. On the outward journey the drift was to starboard; therefore double the drift (20°) must be *added* to give 10° port drift on the return journey (*Fig.* 51).

$$\therefore \quad \begin{aligned} 008° + 20° &= 028° \\ \text{Hdg.(T)} &= 028° \\ \text{Drift} = 028° - 018° &= 10° \text{ P} \end{aligned}$$

AERONAUTICAL MAPS AND CHARTS

By common usage practically any sheet depicting the surface of the earth, regardless of projection, scale or colour, is referred to as a "map," although more correctly a map is a pictorial representation of the ground, whereas a chart is used for areas of water.

It is, of course, not possible to design a map which will be ideal for all purposes. Furthermore the map maker is faced with the impossible task of depicting a spherical shape on a flat surface so that inevitably a degree of distortion must be present in all maps. To a certain extent this may be minimized by showing relatively small areas of the surface of the earth on each map. Conversely maximum distortion may be seen in the usual map of the world printed in a school atlas where an entire hemisphere is printed on a single page.

Various **Projections** (methods of constructing a map) are in common use, each conveying certain information accurately at the expense of other features, since it is impossible to produce a map which accurately portrays distance, direction, shape and area all on one sheet although the ones most widely used for pilot-navigation represent an excellent compromise providing balanced overall accuracy. Aviation maps give prominence to features of most interest to the pilot and these are listed later in the chapter.

Scale. Scale is simply the ratio between distance on the map and the actual distance on the ground. This map/ground ratio can be expressed in three ways—

1. By a representative fraction (r.f.). For example, an r.f. of 1:500,000 means that 1 unit on the map or chart is equivalent to 500,000 units on the ground. Maps of this scale, 1:500,000, are usually referred to as "the half-million series."
2. By graduated scale lines, three of which—statute miles, nautical miles and kilometres—are located at the foot of the map or chart. Additional graduations in these units are sometimes drawn around the margin.
3. By a statement, e.g. $\frac{1}{4}$ *inch to one mile*, which simply means that $\frac{1}{4}$ inch on the map represents 1 mile on the ground.

Maps and Charts for Pilot Navigation. As already mentioned one particular scale of map or chart will not serve every occasion, and the student should be conversant with more than one series of maps although he may hear many pilots claiming that they can find their way anywhere with this or that series of maps.

A popular map for cross-country flying in light aircraft of low cruising speed is the 1 : 250,000 *Series Topographical Air Map of the U.K.* The I.C.A.O. 1 : 500,000 aeronautical charts can also be used for pilot navigation. In poor visibility the 1 : 250,000 is the better map to use as it gives greater detail; in

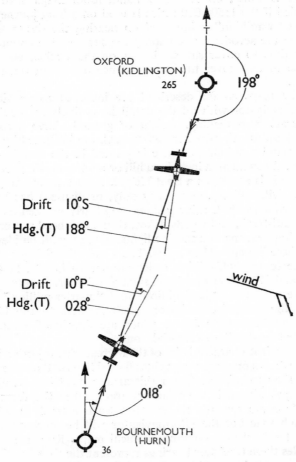

Fig. 51. MAKING GOOD A RECIPROCAL TRACK

good visibility, on the other hand, fewer maps have to be carried if the 1:500,000 series is used on a long journey—the "quarter million" being used on nearing the destination to locate the aerodrome and study the surrounding countryside. The time to cover say six inches on the 1 : 500,000 will be twice that to cover the same distance on the quarter-million map.

The maps so far described are intended to provide the pilot/navigator with all the detail he is likely to require for accurate map reading. Height of ground above **Mean Sea Level** and depth of water below m.s.l. are indicated by **Layer Tints** and a colour reference is printed in the margin of the sheet. When an area includes a hill or mountain of a prominent nature it is shown as a **Spot Height**. Each type of aerodrome (e.g. civil, military, emergency only, or disused) has its own particular symbol, railway lines are clearly marked as single or multi-track, and woods, lakes, rivers, overhead power lines, flashing beacons and marine lights, etc., may all be identified on these **Topographical** maps. The **Conventional Signs** as they relate to the half-million series are shown in *Fig*. 52 (pages 111 and 112). Quarter-million signs are similar. So much detail is present on the "half-million" and "quarter-million" series that the specialist navigator usually prefers to run his **Air Plot** on **Mercator's Charts** which are devoid of colour and limited in detail to essentials only.

One of the characteristics of the Mercator's projection is that a line drawn on these charts cuts all meridians at the same angle. For the specialist navigator this arrangement has certain advantages although the resultant track takes the form of a gentle curve towards the equator. Such a track is called a **Rhumb Line** but the pilot/navigator will be more concerned with tracks drawn on topographical maps. Known as **Great Circles** these tracks or bearings represent the shortest distance from one point on the surface of the earth to another but it should be remembered that they cut each meridian at a slightly different angle (page 77).

With the development of radio navigation special charts have become necessary and in airline and indeed other branches

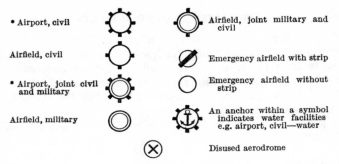

(a) Aerodrome symbols

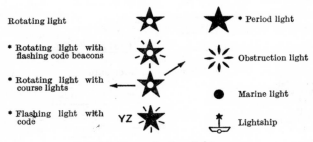

(b) Air navigation lights

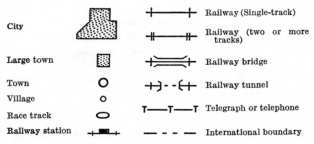

(c) Cultural features

Indicates symbols (now abandoned) which appear on charts published prior Nov. 1951.

Fig. 52. Symbols used on the I.C.A.O.

1 : 500,000 series of aeronautical maps.

of flying these assume prime importance. Those covering a large area are called **Radio Navigation Charts** while **Landing Charts** to a larger scale are available for all international aerodromes equipped with radio aids, a separate chart being provided for each aid and each runway, but the subject of

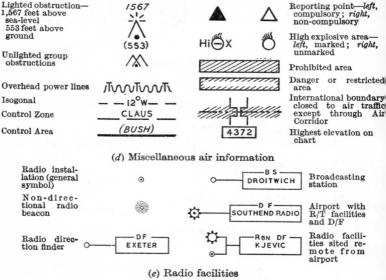

(d) Miscellaneous air information

(e) Radio facilities

Fig. 52 (*cont.*). SYMBOLS USED ON THE I.C.A.O
1 : 500,000 series of aeronautical maps.

radio navigation (fully explained in FLIGHT BRIEFING FOR PILOTS, Vol. III) is best introduced at a later stage in flying training.

Folding a Map. A new map should first be folded in half across its width so as to leave only the face exposed. Next, fold it concertinawise into a double "W"; for smaller maps five hinges may suffice. In this form a map is more manageable in the air and can be quickly stowed into a map pocket; even so, this method will not suit all cross-country flights, for example, the Track may run closely parallel with the centre fold. Another way of arranging the map is the strip method; in this form the Track passes down the centre of the strip. A considerable margin of map on either side of the Track should be included, as landmarks to port or starboard are often more valuable than those lying beneath the actual path of the aircraft which may in fact be hidden by fuselage or wing. Furthermore, pilots have often been embarrassed by searching the map for a feature which has been just the other side of a fold.

To save wear and tear on maps and charts celluloid cases can be used. Large sizes, 16 in. × 12 in., are obtainable from map suppliers as well as government surplus stores. Tracks and observations can be entered on the celluloid with coloured chinagraph pencils. An added advantage with this pencil is the thick Track line it draws—easily visible during momentary glances from ground to map. Heavy lines may be drawn on the map itself with a carpenter's pencil. The lead is soft, so facilitating the erasing of Tracks, a job which should be done after each flight in order to avoid confusion later on.

Time-interval Marks. Timing plays an important part on a cross-country flight, so in order to check on progress along a route by comparing the actual ground-speed with the D.R. ground speed (used when completing the pre-flight log) the Rqd. Tr. is divided into time intervals. Some instructors recommend intervals of five or ten minutes, but this has the disadvantage that some of the check marks, perhaps all, may fall on obscure pin-points on the map; or there may even be no feature at all by which to check ground speed. Consequently, this modified form of marking time intervals possesses certain advantages.

METHOD

(a) Estimate five minutes flying along the Rqd. Tr. and examine the map for a prominent feature over which the Track should pass. Mark this check point with a line drawn at right-angles through the Rqd. Tr.

    (*b*) Draw additional check marks through other conspicuous pin-points at intervals of approximately five minutes flying time.

    (*c*) Measure the distance to the destination and draw a half-way mark.

    (*d*) Accurately measure the distance from the point of departure to each check point and using the D.R. ground speed calculate the time to each check point. This is easy with the aid of the circular slide-rule described earlier. Enter these times against the appropriate marks.

An example in marking time intervals is shown on Map 1 on the inset facing this page; a flight from Ingoldmells to Nether Thorpe. The first check point, a bend in a river, should be used to correct any track error as well as to check ground speed. The other time-interval mark, seven and a half minutes beyond the first, indicates a single-track railway passing at right-angles below the Rqd. Tr.; this provides a good point at which to check the ground speed and revise the E.T.A. at Nether Thorpe. The half-way mark does not lie on a prominent pin-point, but it is close enough to a railway to establish when approximately half the distance has been covered.

It will be noted that 5° lines have been drawn either side of track on Map 1. These assist the pilot to determine track error at the beginning of the flight.

Features to Aid Map Reading

Coastline. This is one of the best features as it is very prominent and easily distinguishable. Many stretches of coastline are unique in shape and bearing, thus the likelihood of confusion is lessened (see Map 2, facing page 115).

Water. Lakes, reservoirs, large rivers, estuaries and canals are likewise valuable map reading features. Water, too, stands out quite clearly in moonlight.

Hills and Mountains. These can be important landmarks, especially when isolated by low-lands, e.g. the Mendip Hills in

Somerset, the Wrekin in Shropshire and, on a larger scale, the York Moors and Wolds. However, lesser hills are not very prominent above 3,000 ft.

Towns. Generally, the smaller the town the easier it is to identify. It should be viewed as a whole and compared with the direction of the rivers, canals, railways and roads which serve it. After the identity of a town has been quite definitely established a particular landmark may help to re-determine its identity at some future date, e.g. a castle (Windsor), cathedral (Durham), station, stadium or housing estate.

City. Map reading over, or near, a large city can be most difficult. Railways and roads are so numerous as to be of little use and suburban towns lie so close to the main mass that it is impossible to view them in a detached way.

Railways. The greater the number of railway lines which lie beneath the Track, the less should the pilot be inclined to trust them. Study the whole visible length of line and its bearing. Observe, too, the junctions, intersections, tunnels, cuttings and embankments. As with all other prominent features, it should be used not as a separate feature but as a patch in the whole quilt of ground detail.

Roads. Quite often they are of little value in the British Isles unless they are unique. Watling Street is a good example of this ideal and motorways are very distinctive.

Woods. Many parts of the country are dotted with small woods; this makes confusion easy. Added to this, cloud shadows on the ground are often mistaken for woods. Large woods make more reliable pin-points, as they are less numerous and more easily recognizable. With extensive areas under reafforestation it is quite possible for a wood to appear on the ground long before the maps can be brought up to date. This applies equally as well to the vast number of new housing estates going up all over the country. Similarly, be wary of uncharted lakes appearing in low-lying areas during rainy periods. To avoid this dilemma of looking on the map for something which is not marked there, read from the *map to the ground* and not from the ground to the map.

Snow. A light fall of snow on the ground can often aid map reading, as the useless mass of small detail is blotted out and the main arteries and landmarks are thrown into greater prominence.

Incidental Aids. On rare occasions during a flight over water it may help on the journeying through the air to know that wind lanes on the surface of the sea are an indication of the wind direction below 1,500 ft. Remember, too, the changing position of the sun during the day, e.g. at noon the sun should be on the port beam when flying on a westerly course.

There are times when knowing the mileage to a distant landmark can be of aid to cross-country navigation. Estimating distances accurately from the air comes only with practice, so to gain proficiency it is a good idea to ring lightly, on a $\frac{1}{4}$-inch map, the home aerodrome with circles two miles apart; up to a limit of about twenty miles radius. Then select prominent landmarks at varying distances from the airfield and note their mileage. In good visibility view these landmarks from different heights above the airfield and use the prepared map to check estimations of the distances. The following table gives distances to the horizon in perfect visibility; the figures in brackets are less accurate but perhaps more easily memorized.

Height of Aircraft	Distance to Horizon
1,000 ft	$38\frac{3}{4}$ miles (40)
2,000 ft	$54\frac{3}{4}$ miles (55)
3,000 ft	$67\frac{1}{4}$ miles (66)
4,000 ft	$77\frac{1}{2}$ miles (77)

Cross-country Flying
In so far as non-radio pilot navigation is concerned successful cross-country flying is dependent upon the following factors—
  1. The ability to read a map.

2. An understanding of the effects of the wind on the aircraft's progress in relation to the ground and how to make allowance for the resultant drift, etc.

3. The accurate use of the compass and watch.

Good map reading like any other form of reading (music, shorthand or even everyday text) will only develop with practice.

How to work out the effects of wind with the aid of a navigational computer was explained earlier in the chapter along with in-flight corrections using the "one-in-sixty" rule.

Accurate course steering is greatly simplified when a **Direction Indicator** (sometimes called a **Directional Gyro**) is fitted but since it must be synchronized with the magnetic compass the behaviour of this basic instrument must be fully understood. While the use of the magnetic compass is fully described on page 81, FLIGHT BRIEFING FOR PILOTS, Vol. I, here are the main considerations which should be remembered when using the instrument—

1. Turns must not exceed Rate 1.

2. When turning on to north roll out of the turn 25–30° early.

3. When turning on to south roll out of the turn 25–30° late.

4. When turning on to east or west allow the aircraft time to stop turning by rolling out 5–10° early.

5. When reading the compass on northerly or southerly headings lateral level must be maintained otherwise the north-seeking end of the compass needle or card will swing towards the lower wing.

6. When reading the compass on easterly or westerly headings the air-speed must be steady. An increase in speed will cause an apparent turn towards north while a decrease in speed will make the compass swing towards south (acceleration and deceleration error).

7. The compass needle or card is sluggish on northerly headings and lively on southerly headings.

8. In the absence of a Direction Indicator accurate course keeping may be achieved by steering towards a distant

cloud or ground feature. Reference to the compass should be made at frequent intervals and the distant point will have to be changed every few miles.

The watch is a vital aid to navigation enabling the pilot to anticipate when a particular feature on the map should appear below the aircraft. During flight time between **Pin-points** on the ground may be related to the circular slide-rule and the resultant ground speed used to confirm or revise the E.T.A.

The background information provided in this chapter may now be applied in practice. Pilot Navigation is an air exercise and as such it is described in Chapter 20, FLIGHT BRIEFING FOR PILOTS, Vol. I.

CHAPTER 4

Air Law

EVERY motorist is familiar with the *Highway Code* and realizes the importance of its application to all road users. It therefore follows that pilots should understand the various regulations which have been designed for the safety of all who fly. Since on occasions airspace is shared by transport and light aircraft many of these regulations are equally applicable to professional and amateur pilot alike and it is primarily these regulations with which this chapter is concerned. In a book of this size aviation law can only be treated in general terms. Most of the information in this chapter is based upon *Aviation Law for Applicants for the Private Pilot's Licence* (C.A.P. 85) which may be obtained from H.M. Stationery Office.

Pilot's Licence
There are five different classes of licence for air pilots and in order of seniority they are

Title	Abbreviation
Airline Transport Pilot's Licence	ATPL
Senior Commercial Pilot's Licence	SCPL
Commercial Pilot's Licence	CPL
Private Pilot's Licence	PPL
Student Pilot's Licence	SPL

Student and Private Pilots' Licences
A person who wishes to obtain a pilot's licence should make application to the Board of Trade, Department of Aviation, Licensing Department, Shell Mex House, Strand, London.

Form SAL 101 must be completed and subject to the results of a medical examination conducted by a local doctor the Department of Aviation will issue the applicant with a Student Pilot's Licence. This entitles the student to fly an aircraft solo under the supervision of a qualified flying instructor but before carrying passengers while in command of an aircraft the candidate must qualify for a Private Pilot's Licence. To obtain this it is necessary to complete a 40-hour course of instruction of which not less than 10 hours will be as pilot in charge. Certain flying schools which reach the required standards have Board of Trade approval to conduct courses reduced to 35 hours' flying provided this is completed within a period of six months. In either case the course culminates in a solo cross-country flight with two intermediate landings over a triangular course, one leg of which must be at least 50 nautical miles' distance from the point of departure. The flying syllabus for the PPL is covered in Volume I of this series. There is a final flight test embracing all basic manoeuvres and a written examination of the "selective answer" type on Aviation Law, Navigation and Meteorology (specimen questions are included in Appendix 1). The examinations include an oral test related to a general knowledge of airframes and engines with particular reference to the type of aircraft flown by the student throughout the course.

The results of these examinations together with a check list of manoeuvres required for the flight test are recorded on the PPL application form SAL 102. Qualified or near qualified service pilots are exempt from the various tests provided the application for a Private Pilot's Licence is supported by the applicant's Squadron Commander or Commanding Officer.

The Private Pilot's Licence is valid for a period of 5 years from date of issue (or renewal). It includes the following certificates—

(a) Personal particulars of holder.
(b) The ratings to which the holder is entitled.
(c) Two certificates relating to experience and periodic checks.

(*d*) Medical certificate which must be renewed every 25 months for holders under 40 years of age and every 13 months thereafter.

Incorporated in the licence is an aircraft rating certificate which is subdivided into three classes of aircraft—

Group A   Single-engined aircraft below
                 12,500 lb maximum total
                 weight authorized
Group B   Multi-engined aircraft
                 below 12,500 lb MTWA
Group C   Aircraft over 12,500 lb MTWA

In order to maintain a group on a PPL every 13 months the holder must produce evidence of 5 hours' in-command flying experience on an aircraft of the same class, his licence and log book being checked by an authorized examiner who, on being satisfied will sign the certificate of experience (mentioned under heading (*c*) in the description of the PPL). When a licence holder has not completed the qualifying 5 hours' flying to maintain a group, retention of that group will be subject to a satisfactory flying test conducted by the examiner.

A PPL entitles the holder to fly passengers, but not for hire or reward, this privilege being reserved for the three professional licences which are now described.

Commercial Pilot's Licence
The requirements for the issue of a CPL are as follows—

1. A total of 700 hours' flying or alternatively 150 hours full-time course of approved training.
2. Adequate flying training under a qualified flying instructor including not less than 10 hours' instruction in instrument flying.
3. At least 100 hours as pilot-in-command of which—

   (*a*) 20 hours will have been cross-country or overseas flying as pilot-in-command including one flight of at least 300 nautical miles during which two intermediate landings and stops will have been made.

(*b*) 10 hours were flight by night during which the applicant completed 10 landings and take-offs without assistance from any other pilot. Of this 10 hours up to half may have been complete under instruction in a dual-controlled aeroplane.

4. At least 10 hours' flying within the six months immediately preceding the date of issue of the licence.

When flying as Captain for hire and reward holders of the CPL are restricted to aircraft not exceeding 12,500 lb maximum all up weight.

Senior Commercial Pilot's Licence

The requirements for the issue of a SCPL are as follows—

1. A total of 700 hours' flying as pilot.
2. Not less than 200 hours' as pilot-in-command which must include the following experience—

    (*a*) at least 50 hours' cross-country or overseas flying of which 10 hours must be at night or on instruments.

    (*b*) at least 15 hours' night flying which is additional to the 10 hours mentioned under (*a*).

    (*c*) at least 10 hours' flying within the six months immediately preceding the date of issue of the licence. (When a first pilot rating is not required 20 hours' co-pilot time will be accepted in lieu of (*c*).)

    (*d*) of the 200 hours mentioned at the beginning of paragraph 2 a maximum of 50 hours may be obtained while acting as captain under the supervision of a qualified pilot-in-command. Two hours' flying under these conditions will count as one hour towards the 50 hours mentioned at the beginning of this sub-paragraph.

3. A reasonable amount of flying experience in the type of aircraft to which the application relates.
4. Not less than 40 hours' instrument flying (actual or with

hoods, etc.) of which up to 20 hours may be completed in an approved simulated flight trainer (e.g. Link).
5. The remainder of the 700 hours may be accumulated as pilot-in-command, co-pilot or as pilot under instruction. Half co-pilot time may be counted towards the total provided the type of aircraft is required to carry more than one pilot. All flying under a qualified flying instructor may be counted.
6. When the applicant for a SCPL has passed an approved course of training the 40 hours' instrument flying mentioned under paragraph 4 may be reduced to 30 hours of which up to 10 hours may be done in an approved simulated flight trainer.

When flying as Captain for hire and reward holders of the SCPL are restricted to aircraft not exceeding 45,000 lb maximum all up weight.

Airline Transport Pilot's Licence
1. Applicants for the ALTP must produce evidence of having flown a total of at least 1,200 hours as pilot.
2. Of the total mentioned in paragraph 1 not less than 250 hours must have been as pilot-in-command and this will include—

   (a) at least 200 hours' cross-country or overseas flying of which 25 hours are at night (or alternatively 100 hours' cross-country or overseas flying which includes 25 hours by night in addition to 200 hours as co-pilot).

   (b) at least 10 hours as pilot-in-command within the six months immediately preceding the date of issue of the licence. (When a first pilot rating is not required 20 hours' co-pilot time will be accepted in lieu of (b).)

   (c) of the 250 hours mentioned at the beginning of paragraph 2 a maximum of 100 hours may be obtained while acting as captain under the supervision of a qualified pilot-in-command. Two hours' flying

under these conditions will count as one hour towards the 100 hours mentioned at the beginning
of this sub-paragraph.

3. At least 100 hours' night flying, either as captain or co-
pilot.
4. At least 75 hours' instrument flying (actual or with hoods,
etc.) of which not more than 25 hours may have been
completed in an approved simulated flight trainer.
5. A reasonable amount of flying in the type of aircraft to
which the application relates.
6. The remainder of the 1,200 hours may be accumulated
as pilot-in-command, co-pilot or as pilot under instruction. The same conditions apply as for the Senior Commercial Pilot's Licence (paragraph 5 under that heading).

There is no aircraft weight limitation on holders of the ATPL.

RATINGS

As knowledge and flying experience increase the private and
professional pilot may obtain the following ratings—

1. Aircraft Rating
2. Night Rating
3. Restricted Radio Telephony Certificate of Competence
4. Flying Instructor's Rating
5. Instrument Rating
6. The IMC Rating

1. Aircraft Ratings

As already explained the PPL entitles the holder to fly aircraft
in any or all of three groups of aircraft types. Almost invariably
the licence is first issued with light single-engined aircraft
privilege (Group A) and a short conversion course will be
necessary before the pilot can attempt the flying test for light
multi-engined types or bigger aircraft weighing more than
12,500 lb for which an Air Registration Board type technical
examination is required.

2. Night Rating

With the exception of flight under the supervision of a qualified flying instructor no pilot may fly at night unless he has a night rating. The requirements for this addition to the PPL are

1. A minimum of 50 hours' flying of which half must be as a pilot in command.
2. A minimum of 5 hours' instruction on instrument flying of which half may have been practised in a simulator (e.g. Link Trainer).
3. A minimum of 5 hours' night flying under the supervision of a qualified instructor in which must be included at least five separate flights as pilot-in-charge, this to be completed within six months of making application for the rating.

3. Restricted Radio Telephony Certificate of Competence

With the development of all types of flying activity it is becoming increasingly necessary for all pilots to be able to communicate with the various air traffic services on the ground. The rapid increase in air traffic has brought with it a similar growth in profusion of radio communications so that brevity in passing information and a knowledge of correct procedures is essential if smooth working of the air traffic control services is to be ensured. The R/T Licence is gained by a practical test which is described in Chapter 5.

4. Flying Instructors' Ratings

Whereas any motorist may teach another person to drive a car, instruction by pilots not qualified as instructors is not admissible by the Board of Trade as qualifying experience for a PPL.

For many years there have been two classes of Flying Instructors' Ratings. Requirements are as follows—

1. *Assistant Instructor's Rating*
   (i) A valid pilot's licence.
   (ii) A minimum of 150 hours as pilot-in-command. This must include at least 30 hours' experience on the class of aircraft to which the application relates.

(iii) Not less than 5 hours' experience in command of the type of aircraft to which the application relates.

(iv) An approved flying instructor's course of 20 hours' duration of which 5 hours will entail instructor practice with another pilot.

Candidates with these qualifications undergo a flying test and an oral examination with a Board of Trade approved examiner.

Holders of the Assistant Flying Instructor's Rating may only instruct under the supervision of an instructor with the more senior rating now described.

2. *Flying Instructor's Rating*

Candidates for this rating must produce evidence of

(i) A valid pilot's licence.

(ii) A minimum of 400 hours as pilot-in-command.
This must include at least 30 hours' experience on the class of aircraft to which the application relates.

(iii) A minimum of 200 instructional hours and six months as an Assistant Instructor or as a qualified service instructor.

Both ratings are confined to day instruction unless the applicant has completed 10 hours' flying by night of which up to five hours may have been dual. Two hours of the dual night flying must have been flown in the seat normally occupied by the flying instructor and in the company of an approved instructor. There is a separate aerobatic rating.

At the few schools training airline pilots, flying instuctors are tested by Board of Trade examiners, all other instructors and instructor candidates being tested by the Panel of Examiners, a small committee of very experienced flying instructors operating within the framework of The British Light Aviation Centre.

5. Instrument Rating

Flying an aircraft over open country on a clear day is within the capabilities of the most inexperienced. Piloting an aircraft through areas of intense traffic under conditions of low cloud and poor visibility is quite a different matter. It will shortly be explained that certain areas of high activity (e.g. the London, Manchester or Paris areas) are of necessity subject to rigid control by the air traffic services. It is imperative that pilots flying within **Controlled Airspace** should be capable of maintaining both height and position to very high standards of accuracy, using the flight instruments and radio aids provided in the aircraft. When the weather deteriorates below certain minima only pilots with an Instrument Rating may fly within controlled airspace and it therefore follows that this is an essential qualification for all pilots engaged on air transport, and a great asset to the non-professional pilot using an aircraft for business purposes.

The requirements for an Instrument Rating are

(i) Completion of an instrument flying course at a Board of Trade approved flying school.
(ii) At least 150 hours' experience of which 50 hours must be cross-country flying as pilot-in-command.
(iii) At least 40 hours' instrument flying of which 20 hours may have been conducted on a simulator.

There is an examination to pass and a stringent flying test which is held with a Board of Trade examiner.

Instrument Flying is explained in Chapter 6 of Volume II and Radio Aids to Air Navigation are dealt with in some detail in Volume III of this series.

6. The IMC Rating

With effect from 1st January 1970 holders of the U.K. Private Pilot's Licence are subjected to certain bad weather restrictions when flying within and outside controlled airspace. The IMC rating may be added to the PPL thus allowing the holder to fly under these conditions:

Outside Controlled Airspace: no limitations.
Within Controlled Airspace: minimum flight visibility $1\frac{1}{2}$ nm (3 km).

Requirements. Candidates for the rating must have at least 100 hours' pilot experience to include 60 as pilot in charge, of which 30 hours are cross-country time. Applicants must hold an R/T licence.

Course. This embraces 10 hours' instrument flying on the full and limited panel and instruction on the use of VHF D/F. Candidates may elect to complete 5 hours' tuition in a Link Trainer or flight simulator when the 10 hours' flight training can be reduced to 8 hours.

Test. During the air test candidates must fly on instruments within certain limits of accuracy. There is an oral examination on the following subjects: flight planning; en-route and approach navigation using VHF D/F and radar; meteorology; altimeter setting procedures; use of the *Air Pilot* and other publications for the planned use of radio facilities; and finally the privileges and limitations of the IMC rating itself.

A fuller explanation of the IMC Rating is contained in Chapter 12, Volume II (third edition). Currently the rating is only valid within the U.K.

GENERAL FLIGHT RULES

Right of Way in the Air

1. Aeroplanes must give way to airships, gliders and balloons.
2. When two aircraft are flying on converging courses, the one which has the other on its starboard side shall give way (*Fig.* 53).
3. When two aircraft are approaching head-on each shall alter course to starboard (*Fig.* 54).
4. An aircraft overtaking another shall alter course to starboard (*Fig.* 55).
5. An aircraft following a railway, coastline or other prominent line feature must fly to the right of such a landmark (*Fig.* 56.).
6. Right of way must be given to an aircraft when it is landing or approaching to land.

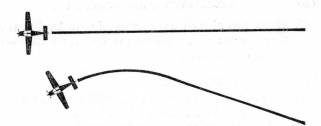

Fig. 53. APPROACHING ON CONVERGING COURSES

Fig. 54. APPROACHING HEAD-ON

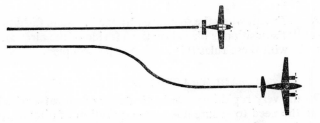

Fig. 55. OVERTAKING ANOTHER AIRCRAFT

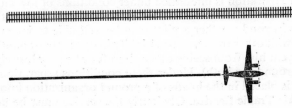

Fig. 56. FOLLOWING A LINE FEATURE

7. When two aircraft are approaching to land at the same time the one which has the greater height must give way to the lower one.

Right of Way on the Ground

1. An aircraft shall not take off until there is no apparent risk of collision. The direction of take-off shall normally be in the direction indicated for landing.
2. An aircraft taxi-ing along a taxi-way or runway shall keep to the starboard side.
3. Right of way shall be given to a vehicle towing an aircraft.
4. A vehicle not towing an aircraft shall give way to aircraft taxi-ing in the vicinity.
5. When two aircraft or an aircraft and a vehicle are approaching head on, each shall alter course to the right.
6. An aircraft overtaking another aircraft or vehicle shall alter course to the left.
7. When two aircraft are taxi-ing on converging courses the one which has the other on its starboard side shall give way.

Note. Except when the seats are arranged tandem fashion the first pilot's position is placed on the left side of the aircraft. To comply with these rules this seat must be occupied.

AIR TRAFFIC CONTROL

With the very rapid increase in air traffic of all categories has come the need to ensure adequate separation of aircraft, particularly over important centres of communication. The importance of separation is intensified under conditions of low cloud and/or poor visibility and a little thought will reveal that whereas in good weather a pilot may be well able to integrate himself with other traffic, poor visibility in one form or another will prevent him from seeing other aircraft or he may lose sight of the ground (or both). Under these conditions separation of aircraft is placed in the hands of a ground organization known as the **Air Traffic Service**. Obviously the service must be kept well informed of the height and position of all aircraft within the area under control. The point at which a pilot may no longer rely upon outside visual references has been clearly defined and the two conditions of flight are known as

Visual Flight Rules   (VFR)
Instrument Flight Rules   (IFR)

Related Weather Conditions
Flight under VFR may only occur under Visual Meteorological Conditions (VMC) and these must allow the pilot to conform to the following limits—

1. At least one nautical mile horizontally and 1,000 ft vertically from cloud and in a flight visibility of at least five nautical miles or
2. When flying outside controlled airspace at altitudes lower than 3,000 ft above mean sea level (a.m.s.l.) the pilot must be clear of cloud and in sight of the surface. Should any of these conditions deteriorate Instrument Meteorological Conditions (IMC) will prevail when the flight must be conducted in accordance with IFR. The following observations will help the student to understand the division of responsibility between pilots and the air traffic service—

   (i) When flying under VFR safe conduct of the flight and separation from other aircraft are the responsibility of the pilot.
   (ii) Irrespective of weather conditions permanent Instrument Flight Rules apply to certain Controlled Airspace.
   (iii) In the United Kingdom flight at night under V.F.R. is not allowed.
   (iv) Non-instrument-rated pilots wishing to fly under the conditions noted in paragraphs (ii) and (iii) are required to obtain a **Special VFR Clearance** which may be granted by the Air Traffic Control Service responsible provided air traffic conditions permit.
   (v) When Instrument Meteorology Conditions prevail pilots wishing to enter Controlled Airspace must

obtain clearance from the appropriate Air Traffic Control (ATC) unit. Clearance will only be granted when

    (*a*) the pilot has an Instrument Rating and
    (*b*) the aircraft is equipped with the appropriate radio communications and navigational equipment.

Within controlled airspace the safe conduct and separation of aircraft flying under IFR is the responsibility of the Air Traffic Service.

CONTROLLED AIRSPACE

Organization and procedure as it relates to air traffic control is to a considerable extent international. In so far as the U.K. is concerned England, Scotland, Wales and Northern Ireland are divided into three **Flight Information Regions (FIR)** which extend from ground to Flight Level 250. Above this level are the **Upper Flight Information Regions (UIR)**. The three FIR/UIRs are known as "Scottish," "Preston" and "London," their position in relation to the British Isles being illustrated in *Fig*. 57. Each FIR/UIR is controlled by an **Air Traffic Control Centre (ATCC)** which provides the following services within the confines of its area—

1. A flight information and alerting service.
2. An air traffic advisory service to aircraft flying under IFR within certain areas and routes.
3. Control of aircraft flying under IFR within the **Airways** and **Control Zones** situated in the FIR.

The various services are available from the Centre on different radio frequencies so that a number of pilots, each operating on a separate frequency may simultaneously call the centre. The FIR/UIR is not controlled airspace although it includes a system of Zones and Airways which are controlled.

Fig. 57. FLIGHT INFORMATION AND UPPER FLIGHT
INFORMATION REGIONS COVERING THE BRITISH ISLES

Control Zones

As already explained certain major airports are subjected to very heavy traffic and it follows that all non-essential flights must be excluded from the circuit and approaches to these major airports which are therefore surrounded by a control zone which usually extends from ground to 11,000 ft level. Often permanent Instrument Flight Rules are adopted within these Control Zones and pilots wishing to fly between two points which are separated by such a zone must either arrange to fly above the upper limit of the controlled airspace, obtain clearance to fly through, or alternatively route the flight around the zone.

Airways

Linking the Control Zones and in effect providing protected corridors between centres of heavy traffic are the Airways. Of ten nautical miles' width the Airways usually extend vertically from a base of 3,000 ft to an upper level of 25,000 ft. Aircraft wishing to cross an airway without entering may fly below its base (terrain clearance permitting) but care should be taken to determine the base of the airway at the point of crossing since the lower limit is stepped down as the airway approaches a junction with a control zone (*Fig*. 58). The Control Zones and their linking Airways are illustrated in *Fig*. 59 fuller details being shown on the relevant aviation charts.

Control Area

Similar to a Control Zone but extending upwards from a specified height above ground level to a maximum height. **Control Areas** occur when a number of airways intersect, typical examples occurring over the London, Manchester and Glasgow areas.

Advisory Service

Although pilots flying outside controlled airspace are responsible for their own separation under IFR conditions they may avail themselves of **Advisory Service** when separation is coordinated by the controlling authority. This service is only

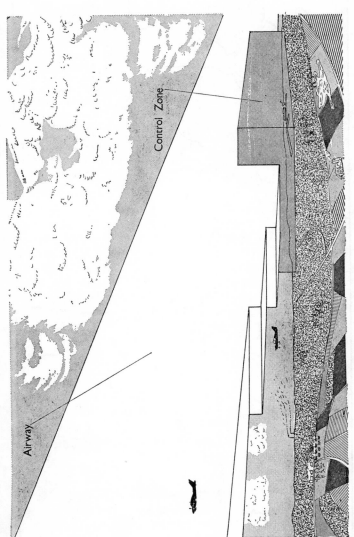

Fig. 58. AN AIRWAY JOINING A CONTROL ZONE

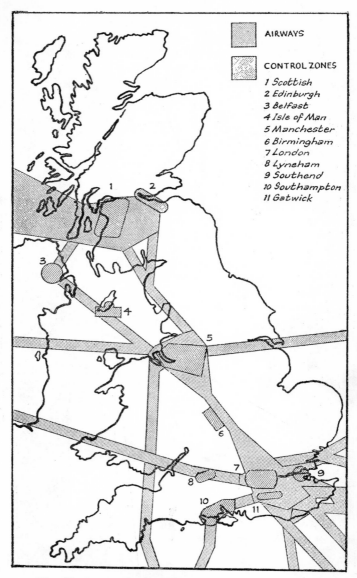

AIRWAYS

CONTROL ZONES
1 Scottish
2 Edinburgh
3 Belfast
4 Isle of Man
5 Manchester
6 Birmingham
7 London
8 Lyneham
9 Southend
10 Southampton
11 Gatwick

Fig. 59. AIRWAYS AND CONTROLLED AIRSPACE WITHIN THE U.K.

available when flying within certain portions of an FIR/UIR known as **Advisory Service Areas**. Some of these areas are in the form of extended corridors when they are known as **Advisory Routes**.

Joint Radar Service Area

This is an upper airspace area where civil and military aircraft are co-ordinated by radar under the control of the joint A.T.C. radar units.

Reporting Points

Although radar coverage of controlled airspace is being extended, to a considerable degree the air traffic service is dependent upon **Position Reports** from captains of aircraft. Without these reports there would exist serious gaps in the overall picture, so making it impossible for the control staff to perform their functions. Therefore all positions of importance to the controllers are designated **Reporting Points** which may either be "mandatory" (shown on aviation charts as solid triangles) or "on request" (outline triangle). Many of these reporting points are marked by a radio facility when a small circle within the triangle is shown on the relevant charts.

Approach Control

The larger airfields provide a local control service for aircraft approaching to land, in transit through the control zone relating to the airfield or during departure from the airfield circuit. Approach control may have at its disposal a radar service. Aircraft wishing to contact approach control would call on the relevant airfield "Approach" frequency.

Aerodrome Control

As the term implies this control unit is concerned with aircraft taxi-ing on the airfield, taking-off and landing and aircraft wishing to use the service would call on the appropriate "Tower" frequency for the aerodrome.

Restricted Areas

For a variety of reasons (e.g. firing practice, target towing, captive balloons, etc.) certain areas are hazardous to aviation and a map of danger areas is available for most countries. In so far as the U.K. is concerned, this may be seen in the *Air Pilot*. The degree of danger may be recognized by the method of marking on the map which is as follows—

1. Solid red outline	Firing, bombing, by day and night, permanently active.
2. Pecked red outline	As above but inactive unless notified by Notices to Airmen (**Notams**), class 1.
3. Solid blue outline	As above but by day only, permanently active.
4. Pecked blue outline	As above, inactive unless notified by Notams, class 1.

In addition to the permanent and semi-permanent danger areas indicated on the map there are also temporary restrictions on flying imposed from time to time, for example during air races, displays and certain public gatherings. Warnings of these restrictions and similar occurrences are given in "Notams," the monthly supplement to the *Air Pilot*, or in Department of Civil Aviation Information Circulars.

Altimeter Setting Procedure

The altimeter is a pressure instrument based upon the principles of an aneroid barometer. Because it is affected by daily pressure changes and alterations in pressure from one area to another the altimeter, its use and limitations are discussed in the chapter on Meteorology on page 61. Bearing in mind that the pilot must rely upon his altimeter for flight separation (i.e. separation from other aircraft) and terrain clearance, the importance of the instrument and the dangers inherent in its misuse should be fully understood.

Flights Outside Controlled Airspace and the Quadrantal Rule

When flying outside controlled airspace or advisory areas pilots must assume responsibility for their separation from other aircraft. Although air traffic outside controlled airspace is of relatively low density the risk of collision with other aircraft is always present and likely to assume greater proportions as each year sees an increase in the number of aircraft registered.

The general flight rules and rights of way have already been explained on page 127 and these by themselves provide a degree of flight separation.

Pilots flying in I.M.C. above 3,000 ft set their altimeters to the standard setting of 1,013·2 mb. This means that above 3,000 ft all aircraft are flown with synchronized altimeters (altimeter setting procedure is explained on page 62). Cruising levels are then chosen according to the aircraft's magnetic track at the time. At first examination it would appear simpler to use compass headings until it is realized that a strong cross-wind will subject a 90K light aircraft to considerable drift whereas a 500K jet aircraft on the same compass heading would be little affected. Although both aircraft may be steering the same compass course they could well be on converging tracks with the attendant risk of collision. Therefore pilots flying outside controlled airspace and above 3,000 ft will achieve separation by

(a) determining their magnetic track and
(b) choosing a cruising level appropriate to that track, using the **Quadrantal Rule,** which in effect divides the compass into four sectors and confines aircraft to certain levels within these sectors.

The quadrantal rule may easily be remembered and is arranged as follows—

Flights between 3,000 ft *and below* 25,000 ft

Magnetic Track	*Cruising Level*
000° to 089° inclusive	Odd thousands of feet
090° to 179° inclusive	Odd thousands of feet + 500 feet
180° to 269° inclusive	Even thousands of feet
270° to 359° inclusive	Even thousands of feet + 500 feet

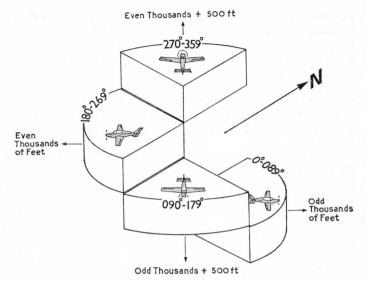

Fig. 60. THE QUADRANTAL RULE AS IT APPLIES UP TO
FLIGHT LEVEL 290

The quadrantal rule as it applies up to flight levels of 29,000 ft
and [the separation achieved are illustrated in *Fig.* 60. Under
the same rule flights at high levels are arranged thus—

Flights at Levels of 25,000 ft *and Above*

Magnetic Track	*Cruising Level*
000° to 179° inclusive	25,000 ft
	27,000 ft
	29,000 ft or higher levels at intervals of 4,000 ft
180° to 359° inclusive	26,000 ft
	28,000 ft
	31,000 ft or higher levels at intervals of 4,000 ft

LOW FLYING

The exhilaration of low flying has a fascination which for some pilots may be likened to the moth and the candle. Although there are certain dangers inherent in low flying it is nevertheless an exercise to be practised under proper conditions and correct supervision. The pilot who understands the principles of low flying is less likely to find himself in difficulty should an emergency occur which can only be resolved by continuing the flight below lowering cloud and in sight of the ground.

Before it is attempted solo, low flying must be carried out under the guidance of a qualified flying instructor. Selected low flying areas are sometimes available for this exercise (explained in Chapter 17, Volume I) but in any event it should be practised over open country free from power cables, television masts, smoke stacks or other obstructions and never near hospitals, houses or farm animals. The law relating to the minimum safe altitude of aircraft is as follows—

(a) An aircraft other than a helicopter shall not fly over any congested area of a city, town or settlement below—

   (i) such height as would enable the aircraft to alight clear of the area and without danger to persons or property on the surface in the event of failure of a power unit, or

   (ii) a height of 1,500 ft above the highest fixed object within a distance of 2,000 ft.

(b) An aircraft shall not fly—

   (i) over or within 1,000 yards of any assembly in the open air of more than 1,000 persons assembled for the purpose of witnessing or participating in any organized event, except with the permission in writing of the Minister and in accordance with any conditions therein specified and with the consent in writing of the organizers of the event; or

   (ii) below such a height as would enable it to alight clear of the assembly in the event of the failure of a power unit.

(*Note*. When a pilot charged with contravention of this subparagraph is able to prove that he flew within the limits mentioned for reasons not connected with the assembly or event, this proof will be regarded as a good defence.)

(*c*) An aircraft shall not fly closer than 500 ft to any persons, vessel, vehicle or structure.

Exceptions. The foregoing shall not apply during—

(*a*) Air racing
(*b*) Flying displays
(*c*) Taking off and landing or practice approaches to landings when confined to airspace normally used for the purpose.
(*d*) Flying to check navigational aids or procedures at Government or licensed aerodromes.
(*e*) Flying as may be necessary to save life. (Written consent of the organizers is required in the case of (*a*) and (*b*).)

SIGNALS

Not all aircraft carry radio and many of the smaller airfields are likewise without radio facilities so that some means of conveying airfield and circuit information must be provided for pilots arriving over the landing area and those on the ground who are about to depart. These functions are performed by the **Signals Area**, a 40 ft × 40 ft hollow white square situated near the control tower. Within the signals area are displayed various signals which are of sufficient size and prominence to be easily seen from the air by pilots crossing the airfield at a height of 2,000 ft or so. The signals area includes a mast on which are hung various signals for the benefit of pilots on the ground. Since the advent of aircraft radio these signals are of less importance than hitherto but they must nevertheless be understood by pilots for the reasons given at the beginning of this section. The various signals are illustrated on the first three colour plates on the front and back endpapers.

Aircraft Navigation Lights

Aircraft cleared for night flying must carry **Navigation Lights** arranged as follows—

> **Red** light on PORT (left) wingtip.
>
> **Green** light on STARBOARD (right) wingtip.
>
> **White** light on TAIL of aircraft.

The lights are designed so that only one colour may be seen at any angle and it is the practice with some light aircraft to carry a three sector light above the fuselage and a similar one below. Angles of vision for the three lights are illustrated on the last of the colour plates on the back endpaper.

Beacons

The larger civil and military aerodromes have a beacon which is arranged to flash the airfield identification signal in morse (green light at civil and red light at service airfields). At a number of service aerodromes when night flying is not in progress the beacon will be coded to flash the letter "S" instead of the normal station identification, thus indicating that in an emergency night landing facilities are available for aircraft in distress.

Visual Signals

The following visual signals are used by Aerodrome Control to regulate the movements of aircraft.

To an aircraft *on the ground*

Intermittent green beam .	Taxi within the manoeuvring area
Steady green beam . .	Take-off
Intermittent red beam .	Taxi clear of landing path immediately
Steady red beam . .	Remain stationary within manoeuvring area
Intermittent white beam .	Return to parking position

To an aircraft *in flight near an aerodrome*

Intermittent green beam .	Return to the aerodrome and wait for permission to land
Steady green beam or green Very signal	Permission to land
Intermittent red beam .	Permission to land cannot be given; land at another aerodrome
Steady red beam or a red Very signal	Landing temporarily suspended; wait

To an aircraft *on a cross-country flight*

A number of black or white smoke-puff projectiles, or white stars bursting at intervals, or an intermittent white beam flashed in the direction of the aircraft	A prohibited area is being approached; alter course immediately
A series of bursting green stars	A prohibited area has been violated; make distress signals and land at nearest aerodrome

From an aircraft in flight the following visual signals may be used

A succession of red Very lights and/or SOS signalled on a lamp	Aircraft in distress
A succession of white Very lights and/or irregular flashes on navigation lights	Aircraft in difficulty which causes it to land
A succession of green Very lights and/or green flashes on Aldis lamp	Aircraft wishes to transmit an urgent message

SAFETY MEASURES

The carriage by aircraft of the following is prohibited—

(*a*) War munitions, including guns, grenades, etc.

(*b*) Dangerous goods, e.g. explosives.

(*c*) An intoxicated person.

Petrol. Petrol and oil must be carried in the approved stowages.

Smoking. Notices permitting or prohibiting smoking must be displayed in all aircraft.

Aerobatics. Aerobatics must not be carried out unless

(*a*) The aircraft has been certified as safe for aerobatics.

(*b*) The pilot is competent to perform the manoeuvres.

(*c*) The aircraft is over open country and clear of Control Zones and Airways.

Parachute Jumping. Descents by parachute may be made

(*a*) When an emergency makes it necessary.

(*b*) When permission has been given by the Minister for demonstrations or practice jumps.

Dropping of Objects. No object shall be dropped from an aircraft unless permission has been received from the Minister.

Safety Precautions Before Flight
Before taking-off a pilot must ensure that

(*a*) The aircraft he is about to fly has been inspected and that the certificate of maintenance is valid.

(*b*) All the equipment, safety devices and instruments necessary for the flight are correctly stowed in the aircraft.

(*c*) The aircraft is properly loaded.

(*d*) Fuel and oil are sufficient for the flight.

(*e*) The wings, tail-plane and control surfaces are free from snow, ice and frost.

(*f*) The flight can be conducted safely with regard to the weather.

(*g*) There is no doubt whatsoever that the aircraft will be able to take-off, carry out the proposed flight and land, all with safety.

Note. Anything which is found to be unserviceable in the aircraft during the flight must be reported on landing.

AIRCRAFT ACCIDENTS

If an aircraft is seriously damaged in an accident, or a technical defect in the aircraft is the cause of an accident, or a person involved in an aircraft accident is killed or injured, it is then the duty of the pilot concerned to report, by telegram, the following details to the Department of Civil Aviation.

(a) The nature of the accident.
(b) The place of the accident.
(c) The date and time of the accident.
(d) The pilot's name.
(e) The nationality of the aircraft, registration marks, owner's name and, when applicable, name of hirer.
(f) When death or injury has occurred, name of person(s) involved.

These details should be sent as soon as possible after the accident, but in all cases within twenty-four hours. He must also inform the local police.

If the accident occurs outside the British Isles a notice in writing is required by the Department of Civil Aviation.

Removal of Aircraft
An aircraft which is seriously damaged in an accident, e.g. has fuselage or main spar broken or controls smashed or damaged by fire, must not be interfered with unless

(a) It is necessary to extricate persons or animals from the wreckage.
(b) Further damage may occur unless it is moved.
(c) The aircraft is a danger or an obstruction to the public.
(d) The authority of the Department of Civil Aviation has been given.
(e) Three days have expired after the notification of the accident.

Passengers' baggage may be taken from a crashed aircraft provided a police officer is present; in the case of an aircraft coming from abroad, a Customs and Excise Officer must also be present.

PERSONAL LOG BOOKS

All pilots are required to keep a personal log book in which the following particulars are recorded—

Personal details.
Date, times and places of arrival and departure of each flight.
Type and registration of aircraft.
Whether pilot in charge, under instruction, second pilot, etc.
Details of exercise (e.g. instrument flying, night flying).
Particulars of any flight test or competency check.

THE FLIGHT PLAN

A pilot may file a flight plan at any time but when it is necessary to co-ordinate the flight with other traffic a flight plan is mandatory. More specifically a flight plan must be completed under the following circumstances—

1. When it is intended to fly in controlled airspace, in IMC or at night (unless a "special VFR clearance" has been obtained).
2. If in VMC the flight is likely to enter controlled airspace which is under permanent Instrument Flight Rules.
3. If the pilot wishes to make use of the air traffic advisory service mentioned on page 134.

When it is intended to fly more than ten miles from the coast, over mountainous country or sparsely populated areas pilots are strongly advised to file a flight plan so that in the event of any circumstance preventing the arrival of the aircraft at its destination, search and rescue action can be set in motion without delay.

Even when a flight plan is unnecessary pilots must inform air traffic control at the aerodrome of departure before commencement of the flight.

CUSTOMS

Carriage of Certificates and Licences

A pilot flying an aircraft within the U.K. is required to carry the following documents—

Pilot's licence
Certificate of Airworthiness
Certificate of Registration
R/T licence covering the radio installation in the aircraft.

If however the flight is to commence and terminate at the aerodrome of departure and does not involve the crossing of a foreign territory then these documents may be kept at the home airfield.

Flights Abroad

A pilot flying abroad is required to have the following documents—

Pilot's licence
Certificate of Airworthiness
Certificate of Registration
Licence covering the radio installation in the aircraft
Passport
Customs carnet or form XS29.
General declaration.

It is also advisable to carry a fuel carnet (fuel credit card issued by the oil companies) and documents relating to vaccinations, etc., if required.

The foregoing information is a summary of some important aspects of aviation law. Students wishing to extend their knowledge of the subject are advised to obtain copies of *The Air Navigation Order* (1966) and *Rules of the Air and ATC Regulations* (1966).

Pilots must keep informed of new regulations as they come into force as well as alterations in the existing regulations. The following publications are available for the purpose from H.M.S.O.

The Air Pilot. A comprehensive volume giving details of aerodromes, radio facilities, air traffic regulations, meteorological services, etc.

The General Aviation Flight Guide. Selected sections from *The Air Pilot*, both publications being amended by monthly issue of new pages. Although less comprehensive than *The Air Pilot* this publication is adequate for the private or business pilot.

Aeronautical Information Circulars. Issued weekly by the Department of Civil Aviation notifying administrative and operation occurrences and obtainable from Aeronautical Information Service, Tolcarne Drive, Pinner, Middlesex.

CHAPTER 5

The Use of Radiotelephony

WITH the increase in air traffic mentioned elsewhere in this book and the development of control zones, controlled areas and airways, most aircraft, large or small, are of necessity fitted with a VHF radio transmitter/receiver (**Transceiver**).

At certain large airports it is not unusual to find pupil pilots on the circuit with large commercial aircraft. Safe conduct of such mixed traffic is made possible by a common controlling authority in contact with each aircraft through VHF radio equipment.

At first hearing the student may very likely consider radio messages to and from aircraft to be terse verbal shorthand and in many ways this is an apt description, the transmissions being composed of figures, letters, abbreviations and code words. In fact letters and figures are frequently used and because misunderstandings may result from foreign pronunciations, static or other interference with reception, an international phonetic alphabet has been devised to avoid confusion—-

A	Alpha	N	November
B	Bravo	O	Oscar
C	Charlie	P	Papa
D	Delta	Q	Quebec
E	Echo	R	Romeo
F	Foxtrot	S	Sierra
G	Golf	T	Tango
H	Hotel	U	Uniform
I	India	V	Victor
J	Juliett	W	Whiskey
K	Kilo	X	X-ray
L	Lima	Y	Yankee
M	Mike	Z	Zulu

0	Zero	5	Fife
1	Wun	6	Six
2	Too	7	Sev-en
3	Tree	8	Ait
4	Fow-er	9	Nin-er

10s, 100s, etc., are spelt out, e.g. 10 is "one zero," 650 is "six fife zero," 25,000 is "two fife tousand."

Establishing Communication

When aircraft have established contact using the five letter registration as a call sign (or in some cases with foreign aircraft, numbers), the first and the last two letters may then be used, for example Golf Charlie Delta as an abbreviated form of G-ABCD. Generally only the last two letters are used i.e. Charlie Delta.

Before transmitting it is essential to listen carefully and ensure that no other transmissions are being made. To transmit over an existing message is to create unnecessary noise and confusion to the inconvenience of all aircraft operating on that frequency. For example, before requesting taxi clearance the radio is switched on and the pilot may ask for a **Pre-flight Radio Check**. He will call the tower on its appropriate frequency using the aircraft call sign, for example: "Birmingham Tower Chipmunk Golf Alpha Bravo Charlie Delta pre-flight check on 118 decimal three." Communication being established the Tower will answer with an abbreviated call sign "Charlie Delta reading you strength four." The **Readability Scale** is interpreted as follows—

1. Unreadable
2. Readable but with difficulty
3. Readable now and then
4. Readable
5. Perfectly readable.

When a service is required the aircraft will normally call it by name, e.g. "London Airways [this is] Golf Alpha Bravo Charlie Delta," or "Birmingham Approach [this is] Golf Alpha

Bravo Charlie Delta"; "London Radar," etc., and the message, known as the text, will follow.

The following phraseology is used in connexion with such messages—

Acknowledge	. .	. Confirm message understood.
Affirmative .	.	. Yes, or permission granted.
Break . .	.	. Indicating clear separation between one part of the text and another or separate message.
Correction .	.	. Indicating alteration to message which was incorrect.
Go ahead .	.	. Proceed with message.
How do you read .		. At what readability scale are you receiving the message.
I say again .	.	. Repetition of message.
Negative .	.	. No, or permission not granted.
Over . .	.	. Transmission ended and reply expected.
Out . .	.	. Transmission ended, no reply expected.
Read back .	.	. Repeat back message as received.
Roger . .	.	. I have received all of your last transmission.
Say again .	.	. Repeat message.
Speak slower	.	. Self-explanatory.
Standby .	.	. Temporary pause in transmission.
That is correct	.	. Self-explanatory.
Verify . .	.	. Confirm accuracy of message.
Wilco . .	.	. Message understood and will be complied with.
Words twice	.	. Send each word twice for clarity.

At the end of the message the pilot must read back to the controlling authority all vital parts of the message such as altimeter settings and air traffic instructions. At all times GMT is used as the time datum.

Priorities and Types of Transmissions

Aircraft flying on a great variety of operations and in all kinds of weather are subjected to ever-changing situations, some routine and others more exacting. Because all radio messages from a number of aircraft cannot be sent and received simultaneously a system of priorities has been evolved.

Obviously a distress call must have priority over any other message or transmission. For this reason transmissions are divided into the following categories—

1. Distress (page 154)
2. Urgency (page 154)
3. Direction Finding (page 153)
4. Flight Safety Messages
5. Meteorological Messages
6. Flight Regularity Messages

Flight safety messages are those which are transmitted by Air Traffic Control, or position reporting by aircraft. Meteorological messages are self-explanatory and flight regularity messages are related to the normal operation of aircraft, for example refuelling, servicing, alterations in schedules, etc.

Aircraft Reporting Procedure
An **Air-rep** consists of three main parts—

1. Information concerning position, altitude and flight conditions
2. Operational information
3. Weather information.

In practice the standard form of an air report is modified in the interest of brevity but the textbook examples given in this chapter will indicate the form of message and phraseology used. When an air-rep is appropriate the initial call to the ground or controlling authority should provide the following information—

1. Callsign and aircraft type
2. From—to
3. Altitude/flight level
4. Position and/or estimated time to next reporting/check point.

For example—
"London Information, Golf Alpha Bravo Charlie Delta, Commanche from Oxford to Glasgow, flight level six zero, estimating

Birmingham Zone boundary at five seven." From this in-formation the aircraft's identification, type (important since from this the approximate air-speed is known), its height and relative position are made clear.

The Practical Application of VHF

When an aircraft wishes to fly cross-country there are innumer-able services at its disposal. Clearly it would be impossible to have a large number of services on one frequency because many aircraft may require them at once. To reduce congestion to an acceptable level, these services (e.g. Approach-Control, Radar, Flight information, Airways, etc.) are obtained on specific frequencies and it is therefore advantageous to have compre-hensive VHF equipment with multi-channel selection. It is not unusual for a light aircraft to have as many as 360 channels, with frequencies spaced at intervals of 50 kc/s or less.

The correct frequencies for each service may be found in the *Air Pilot* or on a **Radio Facilities Chart** (i.e. a map of the country showing the various ground stations/airfields together with their related frequencies).

The services are simply obtained by selecting the appropriate frequencies (operation of radio transceivers is explained in Volume III, of this series, Chapter 3). The pilot can receive numerous services such as a time check or weather report from almost any airfield during the flight, at the same time enjoying the safety that is afforded by control from the ground.

Although flights outside airways and controlled airspace are not so rigidly controlled, the fact that a pilot reports his flight details to the Flight Information Region means that other pilots flying in the area are aware of his movements, so con-tributing to the general safety of air traffic outside airways, etc.

The **Direction-finding** facilities make a valuable contribution to navigation and a pilot may obtain courses to steer to reach the destination airfield even at a range of 100 miles. After com-munications have been established this information is obtained by requesting D/F (Direction Finding) using the "Q" Code shown at the end of this chapter, although this is by no means mandatory. VHF D/F is explained in Chapter 4 of FLIGHT BRIEFING FOR PILOTS, Volume III.

In addition there is an expanding radar coverage which can give an aircraft's position almost instantaneously and with very great accuracy, a service clearly of immense value to an aircraft in distress. Furthermore it is possible to obtain a highly accurate let down when the ground station is equipped with radar. Various types of equipment are in current use but in principle the ground controller informs the pilot of his relationship to the runway, giving him courses to steer and descent paths to achieve in such a way as to bring the aircraft within a few feet of the end of the runway, and on the centre line. (Radar Approaches, Chapter 9, Volume III.)

Emergency

One of the most vital functions of R/T procedure is that information concerning flight safety can be passed to the appropriate ground station. A prime example of this is when an emergency makes it necessary for an aircraft to transmit a distress call.

Emergency calls may be considered under two headings, namely Distress and Urgency.

The distress call is prefixed by the code words **Mayday-Mayday-Mayday**. This indicates that the aircraft is in imminent danger and requires immediate assistance.

Urgency communications (prefixed by the code **Pan-Pan-Pan**) are those which concern the safety of the aircraft, for example an undercarriage fault on a passenger aircraft would concern the safety of the aircraft but would not mean that it was in imminent danger, as opposed say, to an aircraft on fire, which would clearly produce a situation of very grave and imminent danger.

The Distress Call

"Mayday" spoken three times, "Golf Alpha Bravo Charlie Delta" repeated three times, "Transmitting (e.g.) on 119 decimal 7" followed by the distress message, which should include this information—

Nature of distress
Assistance required
Position of aircraft in distress
Time
Height or flight level
Heading
Air-speed
Any information which may assist rescue

Having made this call on the frequency in use, after a suitable pause (say fifteen seconds) the pilot should change to the **International Distress Frequency** (121·5 Mc/s) and repeat the full distress call. If for any reason the cause of the emergency no longer exists it would be necessary to cancel the distress call. For example, "Mayday Golf Alpha Bravo Charlie Delta cancel distress, fire now extinguished, continuing to Manchester." This call is acknowledged by the controlling ground station, who will, in order to resume normal communications, inform other aircraft that the distress traffic has ended. The aircraft will then revert to the original frequency on which the distress call was made and cancel the distress call on that frequency. The cancellation procedure is important since after the "Mayday" call other aircraft will maintain radio silence until advised **Distress Traffic Ended**.

In certain circumstances it may be necessary for an aircraft to give assistance to another aircraft transmitting a Mayday distress call, e.g. in the event of the call not being acknowledged. The assisting aircraft would use the prefix "Mayday Relay" spoken three times, "This is Golf Alpha Bravo Charlie Delta, etc." (passing the call sign of the distressed aircraft details).

The Examination for the Flight Radiotelephony (Restricted) Certificate of Competency

The purpose of this test is to ensure that those who use radiotelephony equipment on board an aircraft can operate it efficiently and are aware of the correct procedure so that the general flow of R/T traffic is not impeded. It is important that reporting procedures are standardized and that the correct priorities with regard to messages are observed. As explained on page 125 pilots using radiotelephony must be in possession of a Flight Radiotelephony (Restricted) Certificate of Competency. The basis for the necessary examination is a thorough knowledge of CAP 46, Radio Telephony Procedure (obtainable from H.M. Stationery Office). Candidates are advised to study this pamphlet if they wish to pass the examination. Many schools and clubs have some form of simulator where students can get practice in sending messages, a valuable aid towards the issue of a certificate.

The examination takes the form of a written and oral test, based on CAP 46, the oral examination being designed to ensure that the required practical standard has been achieved.

While the following exercise is not intended to be a replica of the R/T text it will nevertheless provide the student with a guide to the form the examination will take.

Brief. You are the Captain of a Dove G-AXYZ flying from Birmingham to Manchester on Airways. The flight plan has been filed and you are required to make those calls necessary for the safe and efficient operation of the aircraft during its flight, and to comply with the requests from the examiner and ground stations (these are invariably fed into a tape recording, which also provides background noises).

Exercise. To check the equipment call

"Birmingham Tower Golf Alpha X-ray Yankee Zulu Preflight check on 118 decimal 3."
"Golf Yankee Zulu reading you strength 5 over."
"Golf Yankee Zulu strength 5 also—out."

If carried, this call should be made on the secondary VHF to establish correct functioning of the equipment.)

> "Birmingham Tower, Golf Alpha X-ray Yankee Zulu, taxi clearance."
>
> *"Golf Yankee Zulu is cleared to holding point, runway three four, QFE 1,013 QNH 1,010."*

Yankee Zulu will acknowledge the air traffic instructions reading back the altimeter setting and concluding with the aircraft callsign, in this case Yankee Zulu.

> *" Yankee Zulu, your airways clearance."*
> "Yankee Zulu ready to copy."

(This means that the pilot will take a mental or written note of the airways clearance.)

> *"Golf Alpha X-ray Yankee Zulu, cleared from Birmingham to Manchester, via Lichfield, Amber 1, to climb and maintain flight level six zero.*

Aircraft repeats back clearance. Birmingham says

> *"Golf Yankee Zulu clear to line up."* (i.e. on the runway).

When ready

> "Yankee Zulu ready for take off."
> *"Golf Yankee Zulu, clear take off, surface wind 330° 10 kt."*

As aircraft climbs away Birmingham calls

> *" Yankee Zulu call Birmingham Approach 118 decimal 05."*

Aircraft calls

> "Yankee Zulu changing frequency to 118 decimal 05 out."

Aircraft calls

> "Birmingham Approach, Golf Alpha X-ray Yankee Zulu, passing through 2,500 ft."

Reply

> *"Golf Alpha X-ray Yankee Zulu call passing through flight level four zero."*

Aircraft calls

> "Birmingham Approach, Wilco."

As the aircraft goes through four zero the pilot calls

> "Golf Yankee Zulu passing through flight level four zero."

Birmingham reply

> *"Golf Yankee Zulu contact Preston Airways on 125 decimal 5."*

Reply

> "Golf Yankee Zulu changing frequency to 125 decimal 5 out."

Aircraft changes to correct frequency, listens and calls

> "Preston Airways, Golf Alpha X-ray Yankee Zulu."
> *"Golf Alpha X-ray Yankee Zulu, Preston Airways, pass your message."*

Aircraft calls

> "Preston Airways, Golf Yankee Zulu, Dove from Birmingham to Manchester, airborne Birmingham at one zero, climbing to flight level six zero, estimating Lichfield two one."

Reply

> *"Golf Yankee Zulu, Roger, call passing Lichfield Beacon."*

The pilot will make a position report here as this is a mandatory reporting point.

Aircraft calls

> "Preston Airways, Golf Yankee Zulu, Lichfield two one, flight level six zero, estimating Congleton three four—over."

At this point sheets of flame are seen coming from the cabin, the pilot operates the fire extinguisher but cannot put out the fire, he calls

> "Mayday Mayday Mayday, this is Golf Alpha X-ray Yankee Zulu, Golf Alpha X-ray Yankee Zulu, Golf Alpha X-ray Yankee Zulu, Dove uncontrollable fire in cabin. Request radar assistance for return to Birmingham. Now three miles north of Lichfield, flight level six zero turning on to one eight zero, speed 145 knots."

The pilot changes frequency to 121·5, (the International Distress frequency) and repeats the call in full. Birmingham acknowledge and the aircraft is turned on to a radar heading to bring it back to Birmingham. However, for the purpose of the exercise the fire which has burnt a hole in the cabin roof, is put out by the slipstream. The aircraft calls

> "Golf Alpha X-ray Yankee Zulu, cancel distress call, fire now extinguished proceeding to Manchester, request permission to rejoin Airway at Lichfield, flight level six zero."

Birmingham approach cancels distress traffic calling all stations

> "*Normal transmissions may be resumed, distress traffic ended.*"
> "*Golf Yankee Zulu is cleared to resume flight to Manchester, call Preston Airways on 125 decimal 5 over.*"

Aircraft replies

> "Golf Yankee Zulu changing frequency to 125 decimal 5 out."

Aircraft calls

> "Preston Airways, Golf Alpha X-ray Yankee Zulu, cancel distress call, fire now extinguished."

Preston acknowledge. Aircraft calls

> "Golf Yankee Zulu proceeding to Manchester estimating Beacon three one Flight level six zero."

Preston reply

> *"Golf Yankee Zulu, call passing Lichfield."*

Aircraft   "Yankee Zulu, Wilco."

Overhead Lichfield aircraft calls

> "Golf Yankee Zulu, overhead Lichfield three one, flight level six zero, estimating Congleton four two."

Preston acknowledge. At this point the pilot considers the fire may have caused some damage to the electrical circuit which is affecting his radio aids and he decides to obtain a true bearing from a nearby station. He calls

> "Preston Airways, Golf Yankee Zulu, requesting permission to leave this frequency to obtain a DF bearing from Castle Donington."
>
> *"Yankee Zulu, affirmative, call when resuming this frequency."*
>
> "Yankee Zulu Wilco, changing frequency to 123 decimal 5 out."
>
> "Castle Donington Approach this is Golf Alpha X-ray Yankee Zulu requesting Quebec Tango Echo (true bearing)."
>
> *"Golf Yankee Zulu your QTE is 325° class Alpha."*

This relates to the accuracy of the bearing (see footnote).

"Golf Yankee Zulu 325°.

after a moment's pause to ensure that the bearing repeated back was correct (if not the DF station would reply, "Negative, I say again.") the aircraft continues the call

"Changing frequency to Preston Airways, out."

"Preston Airways Golf Alpha X-ray Yankee Zulu resuming Airway frequency 125 decimal 5."

Preston acknowledge and moments later the aircraft reports overhead Congleton. Airways reply

"*Golf Yankee Zulu call Manchester Approach on 119 decimal 4.*"

"Yankee Zulu, Wilco, changing frequency to Manchester Approach 119 decimal 4, out."

"Manchester Approach, Golf Alpha X-ray Yankee Zulu, passing abeam Congleton, flight level six zero."

Manchester reply

"*Roger Golf Alpha X-ray Yankee Zulu, descend now to 2,500 ft QNH 1,012 for radar approach to runway two four.*"

"Golf Yankee Zulu leaving flight level six zero for 2,500 ft on QNH 1,012 mb."

Manchester call

"*Golf Yankee Zulu Manchester weather 4 octas 700 ft, 8 octas 1,300 ft. Visibility 4 km. Wind 290 at 15 kt. Runway in use 24 QNH 1,012. QFE 1,003 mb.*"

Note—Class *A* accurate to +— 2°
Class *B* accurate to +— 5°
Class *C* accurate to +— 10°

Aircraft acknowledges the altimeter settings resetting the QNH after passing the transition altitude.

> "*Golf Yankee Zulu contact Manchester Radar, 119 decimal 05.*"
>
> "Golf Yankee Zulu Roger, changing frequency to 119 decimal 05 out."
>
> "Manchester Radar Golf Alpha X-ray Yankee Zulu."
>
> "*Golf Alpha X-ray Yankee Zulu this is Manchester Radar you are identified 6 miles North East of Congleton, turn on to heading zero one five and descend to 1,500 ft QFE 1,003.*"

A series of headings is passed to the pilot which results in the aircraft being brought on a Radar PPI continuous descent approach to land at Manchester.

The preceding text is an example of the type of exercise that the candidate will be asked to complete. It will involve the routine calls necessary for the aircraft to pre-check the VHF equipment, manoeuvre on the ground, obtain take-off clearance, airways reporting procedures and direction finding. It will most certainly include a distress call and it may even be that the pilot is first engaged in an urgency call in the middle of which he is obliged to make a distress call.

Be ready for the unexpected and when the workload builds up think before transmitting; if estimates are required which have not yet been worked out, don't guess, use "standby" or other of the standard phrases which may be regarded as the "tools of the trade."

Finally, practice on a simulator. Construction, utilizing headsets and microphones is simple and within the capabilities of most amateur electricians. Practice on the simulator is time well spent, for not only will it produce a good working knowledge of the subject but it will give confidence and fluency.

Examples from the "Q" Code

QDM   Magnetic course to reach the station with zero wind.
QDR   Reciprocal of QDM.
QFE   Aerodrome pressure (altimeter reads zero on landing).
QNH   Barometric Pressure reduced to mean sea level. (Altimeter reads aerodrome height a.m.s.l. on landing.)
QSY   Changing frequency to – – – – –
QTE   True bearing from station to aircraft.

Specimen Examination Questions

NAVIGATION

1. What R.A.S. would result in a T.A.S. of 120 kt at a height of 8,000 ft, temperature −8°C. ?
2. Given track 090° (T), T.A.S. 115 kt, W/V 270/25 kt what is the true heading?
3. How much fuel is required for a flight of 195 n.m. at a ground speed of 110 kt? If consumption is 19 g.p.h. and a reserve of 12 gallons is to be carried?
4. Given a Hdg.(T) of 179° (T) Variation 9°E, Deviation 2°W what is the compass course?
5. A set of steel-shafted golf clubs placed near the compass would affect—

   (a) The deviation.
   (b) The variation.
   (c) Neither.

METEOROLOGY

1. A westerly wind is blowing over a range of hills running north/south, crossing these hills on a heading of 090° where would you expect to find down currents?

   (a) On the windward side.
   (b) Leeward side.
   (c) Midway.

2. Fog may occur under the following conditions—

   (a) Cold land area, humid air mass, light variable winds.
   (b) Warm land area humid air mass, still air.
   (c) Industrial air pollution, cold land area, light variable winds.

3. When the predominant inference is a ridge of high pressure over the country the weather may be expected to be—

   (a) Gusty winds and frequent squally showers.
   (b) A pleasant fine day with light variable winds.
   (c) Continuous precipitation for most of the day.

4. In an anticyclone the winds blow—

    (*a*) Clockwise in the northern hemisphere.
    (*b*) Clockwise in the southern hemisphere.
    (*c*) Anticlockwise in the northern hemisphere.

AIR LAW

1. An intermittent red beam directed to an aircraft in flight near an aerodrome means—

    (*a*) More than one direction of take-off and landing is permissible.
    (*b*) Permission to land cannot be given.
    (*c*) Circle the airfield until permission to land can be given.

2. Port and starboard navigation lights should be visible in the horizontal plane through an angle of—

    (*a*) 70°
    (*b*) 90°
    (*c*) 110°.

3. A flight plan may be filed at any time by the pilot of an aircraft but it is mandatory to do so—

    (*a*) If the pilot wishes to carry out aerobatics.
    (*b*) When it is intended to fly in controlled airspace.
    (*c*) When it is intended to fly over the sea.

4. In the event of overshoot procedure being carried out at an airfield outside controlled airspace the altimeter setting to be used is—

    (*a*) The airfield QFE.
    (*b*) QNH.
    (*c*) Standard altimeter setting.

5. When climbing through the transition altitude the pilot would reset his altimeter to—

    (*a*) Regional QNH.
    (*b*) QFE.
    (*c*) Standard altimeter setting.

6. At military airfields identification beacons normally flash—

    (*a*) 2 letter morse group in green.
    (*b*) 2 letter morse group in red.
    (*c*) 2 letter morse group in white.

ANSWERS

Navigation

1. R.A.S. 108 kt
2. Hdg.(T) 090°
3. 46 gallons
4. Co. (C) 172°
5. (*a*)

Meteorology

1. (*b*)
2. (*a*)
3. (*b*)
4. (*a*)

Air Law

1. (*b*)
2. (*c*)
3. (*b*)
4. (*a*)
5. (*c*)
6. (*b*)

APPENDIX 2

Weather Chart Symbols

The table below illustrates the symbols used to compile the Station Model (*Fig.* 19, page 51) and their meaning is explained in the cross-reference index that follows.

No.	1	2	3	4	5	6	7	8	9	10
Cloud Amount	○	◔	◓	◕	◑	⊕	◕	◖	●	⊗
Low Cloud	△	⌒	♇	⌒	⌣	– – –	—			
Medium Cloud	∠	⫞	∿	⟋	⟋					
High Cloud*	⌐	⌐⌐	⟋	⌐	⟋					
Past Weather*	○	◐	◑	⚡	☰	❡	●	✳	▽	⤵
Barometer Tendency	⟋	⟋	⤳	⟋	⟍	⟍ ※	⤸ ※	⤳ ※	⟍ ※	⤫ ※
Present Weather	△	∞	∀	⌇	○	∽	⚡			
Fronts	⟩	⟨	⟩	⟩	⟩	⟨	⟩	▨		
*Entered in Red	DIRECTION OF MOTION ⟶									

TOTAL AMOUNT OF CLOUD
1. Clear sky, no clouds.
2. $\frac{1}{8}$ of sky covered.
3. $\frac{2}{8}$ of sky covered.
4. $\frac{3}{8}$ of sky covered.
5. $\frac{4}{8}$ of sky covered.
6. $\frac{5}{8}$ of sky covered.
7. $\frac{6}{8}$ of sky covered.

8. $\frac{7}{8}$ of sky covered.
9. $\frac{8}{8}$ sky completely covered.
10. Sky obscured owing to darkness, fog, blowing dust or sand, or other similar phenomena.

FORM OF LOW CLOUD
  1. Cumulus.
  2. Towering cumulus.
  3. Cumulonimbus without anvil head.
  4. Cumulonimbus, active, with anvil head.
  5. Stratocumulus.
  6. Low clouds of bad weather, e.g. nimbostratus.
  7. Stratus.

FORM OF MEDIUM CLOUD
  1. Thin altostratus.
  2. Nimbostratus or thick altostratus.
  3. Altocumulus.
  4. Heaped altocumulus.
  5. Two layers of altocumulus or altocumulus and altostratus.

FORM OF HIGH CLOUD
  1. Wisp of cirrus.
  2. Patches of thick cirrus.
  3. Tasselled cirrus spreading back into thickening knots of cirrus.
  4. Cirrostratus.
  5. Cirrocumulus.

PAST WEATHER
  1. Fair, clear weather.
  2. Changing cloud conditions.
  3. Large amount of cloud.
  4. Dust- or sand-storm.
  5. Fog or greatly reduced visibility.
  6. Drizzle.
  7. Rain.
  8. Snow.
  9. Showers.
  10. Thunderstorms.

BAROMETRIC TENDENCY
  1. Rising then falling.
  2. Rising then steady.
  3. Rising unsteadily.
  4. Rising steadily.
  5. Falling, then rising more quickly.
  6. Falling, then rising.

7 and 8. Falling unsteadily.
9. Falling steadily.
10. Steady or rising, then falling.

PRESENT WEATHER
1. Hail.
2. Haze.
3. Squalls.
4. Smoke, reduced visibility.
5. Clouds developing.
6. Freezing rain or drizzle.
7. Heavy thunderstorm with rain and/or snow.

FRONTS
1. Cold front at surface level.
2. Cold front aloft.
3. Warm front at surface level.
4. Warm front aloft.
5. Warm and cold fronts occluded, at surface level.
6. Occluded front aloft.
7. Stationary front at surface level.
8. Area of continuous rain.

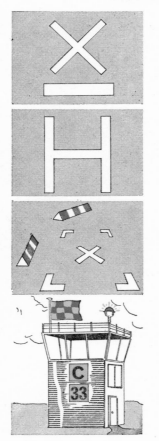

When this sign is painted on the end of the runway land only in emergency. A cross without the bar means runway unfit for use.

Displayed on grass or hard surface this sign indicates the centre of a helicopter landing area. A smaller "H" will also be displayed within the signals area to denote helicopter flying in progress.

Orange/white tent strips alternating with orange/white flags mark bad ground to be avoided while taxi-ing. Airfield or other boundaries may be marked with the orange and white tent strips illustrated.

Chequered flag (or board) denotes aerodrome control is operated by special signals. Letter C marks pilots reporting point. Two figures give direction of take-off and landing (magnetic) to nearest ten degrees. These figures are usually painted on the duty runway or in the case of grass airfields, on the landing and take-off strip in use at the time.